Publishers: Joseph J. Bannon and Peter L. Bannon
Director of Sales and Marketing: M. Douglas Sanders
Director of Development and Production: Susan M. Davis
Technology Manager: Christopher Thompson

ISBN print edition: 978-1-57167-499-9
ISBN ebook: 978-1-57167-666-5
LCCN:2002115243

Sagamore Publishing LLC
1807 N Federal Dr
Urbana, IL 61801

www.sagamorepub.com

Assistive Devices, Adaptive Strategies, and Recreational Activities for Students with Disabilities

A Practical Guide for Including Students
Who Need Assistive Devices and Adaptive
Strategies into Physical Education and
Recreation Activities

by
Buzz Williams

Sagamore Publishing LLC

To my father,

Walter Leonard Williams Sr.,

for challenging me

to find meaningful work

that changes the world—

even if it happens one student

at a time

-B.W.

CONTENTS

Features vii
Acknowledgments ix
Preface xi

PART 1: Adapt, Improvise, and Overcome

Chapter 1: **Introduction** 3
How to Use This Book
The Growing Need
Meeting the Need
Philosophy

Chapter 2: **The Learner** 7
Federal Handicapping Conditions
Degree of Disability
Educational Domains

Chapter 3: **The Teacher** 15
Individual Preparatory Inclusive (IPI) Inclusion Model
Progressive-Competitive-Levels (PCL) Strategy
The Cycle of Change Model

Chapter 4: **Adapting the Environment and Task** 23
Environmental Factors
Task Factors
Primary Competitive Adaptations (PCA's)

Chapter 5: **Improvising Equipment** 29
Traditional Equipment
Alternative Equipment
Fabricated Equipment

PART 2—Application Physical Education and Recreation Activities

Chapter 6: **Basketball** 37
Adapting the Environment and Task
Improvising Equipment
IPI Inclusion Model
Primary Competitive Adaptations
Progressive Competitive Levels Sport Sequence
Case Studies
Activities Chart

Chapter 7: ***Volleyball*** 49
    Adapting the Environment and Task
    Improvising Equipment
    IPI Inclusion Model
    Primary Competitive Adaptations
    Progressive Competitive Levels Sport Sequence
    Case Studies
    Activities Chart

Chapter 8: ***Soccer*** 61
    Adapting the Environment and Task
    Improvising Equipment
    IPI Inclusion Model
    Primary Competitive Adaptations
    Progressive Competitive Levels Sport Sequence
    Case Studies
    Activities Chart

Chapter 9: ***Tennis*** 73
    Adapting the Environment and Task
    Improvising Equipment
    IPI Inclusion Model
    Primary Competitive Adaptations
    Progressive Competitive Levels Sport Sequence
    Case Studies
    Activities Chart

Chapter 10: ***Baseball*** 87
    Adapting the Environment and Task
    Improvising Equipment
    IPI Inclusion Model
    Primary Competitive Adaptations
    Progressive Competitive Levels Sport Sequence
    Case Studies
    Activities Chart

References & Resources 97

Index 99

Features of this Book

Overview of Special Education Terms Related to Physical Education and Recreation
- Federal Handicapping Conditions, their acronyms, and numerical codes
- Mild, Moderate, and Severe degrees of disability
- Educational Domains

IPI Inclusion Model for Physical Education and Recreation
- A practical, "Real-World," model designed for including students with disabilities in physical education, sports, and recreation.

Case Studies for Including Students With Special Needs into Physical Education and Recreation Activities
- Follow case study students Liz, Kevin, Maggie, and Phil, as they demonstrate by example how to implement the practical strategies and methods for each sport and recreational activity.

Progressive-Competitive-Level Sport Sequences for Physical Education and Recreation Activities
- Each sport includes a Progressive-Competitive-Level sequence that provides a ready-made developmental progression for students with varying abilities.

Primary Competitive Adaptations (PCA's) for Physical Education and Recreation Activities
- Each sport includes a description of how each of the three Primary Competitive Adaptations are used to include students with disabilities in competitive activities.

Instructions for building six Pieces of Equipment Every Physical Education and Recreation Inventory Needs
- Each sport includes a description of Traditional and Alternative equipment.
- Instructions included for building six pieces of "Universal Fabricated Equipment".

Physical Education and Recreation Activity Charts
- Each sport includes an activity chart for quick and easy reference to the scope of activities recommended with respect to degree of disability.

Instructional Principles for Adapting and Improvising
- These highlight key points for maximizing student success.

Ready-to-Use Strategies, Activities, and Equipment, Organized by Sport
- Internet Web Site Resources
- Professional Organizations
- Equipment Suppliers & Catalogs
- Disabled Sports Organizations

Acknowledgments

This book is a compilation of lessons learned while teaching at the Kennedy Krieger Institute Schools in Baltimore, Maryland. I would like to thank all of the staff and administrators who have helped me to learn and grow in a nurturing professional environment—Dr. Eddie Denning, Dr. Mary Ellen Lewis, Mr. Arthur Hill, Dr. Robin Church, and Dr. Michael Bender. I am also indebted to Gabrielle Miller and Linda Brandenburg, two colleagues who inspire me to be the best professional I can be.

I would also like to thank the undergraduate students from Towson University who have volunteered hundreds of hours to assist with quality physical education programming. A special thanks to my mentor and friend, Dr. Andrea Boucher, without whom I may have never found my life's work.

The students of the Kennedy Krieger Schools deserve special credit for trusting me, laughing with me, and field-testing all of the wacky inventions and devices to which I introduced them. Their courage in the face of adversity serves to inspire all who have been fortunate to witness it.

A very special thanks to my wife, Gina, and son, Tyler, who have been supportive and understanding of the time and personal sacrifice that writing a book demands.

Preface

I grew up around wheelchairs. My father was the 11th child born of 12 brothers, all of whom, except for my dad, developed a paraplegia affecting both legs—leaving them wheelchair-dependent by age 30. My earliest memories include my uncles and their chairs. I did not realize at the time, but my observations and interactions with my uncles created a unique perspective and philosophy that I would carry with me throughout my personal and professional life. The following are four such memories from my childhood, and the philosophical beliefs that I gained as a result of each experience.

Improvisation is an Equalizer

Uncle Nick

It never bothered me because I never thought of it as a sad place. Manor Care was an adult residential care facility where Uncle Nick lived. He was the youngest of the brothers, but complications with his paraplegia required comprehensive medical care. On one of our weekly trips to visit Uncle Nick, he and dad told nostalgic stories of their youth. Uncle Nick began bragging about being the strongest of all the brothers. There was no doubt he was one of the most handsome—and the most flirtatious. He called to one of the nurses as she passed by, and she stopped. They always did for Uncle Nick.

"Sue, ain't I the strongest in this place?"

"So you say, Nicholas, at least once a day...sometimes more!" She smiled as she winked at me and dad. Uncle Nick took advantage of the audience.

"So when are we going to have lunch together?"

Sue fired back, "When are you going to see how strong you are?"

Uncle Nick maneuvered his chair backward and then quickly jerked it forward, thrusting the two front wheels upward. He rolled to the window on the back wheels and pulled the curtain back.

"See that manhole cover in the parking lot there. I used to be able to pick that up out of the street with one hand. Won a lot of bar bets that way."

The nurse teased as she turned to leave, "We'll have lunch when you pull that out of the street with one hand." Chuckling she added, "I'll be in my office if you need me, Nicholas."

Uncle Nick motioned for us to follow him as he wheeled into the parking lot. I asked dad what he was up to. He told me to watch and learn. Uncle Nick leaned to one side as he removed his leather belt. Then he asked me to reach in through the wide opening of the storm drain and insert the tip of the belt through the quarter-size manhole plate. He grabbed the tip of the belt as it poked through, and pulled until the buckle caught on the underside of the plate. Then he centered himself over the steel plate, and curled the steel plate right out of the ground and onto his lap. With both arms free he wheeled over to a window on the side of the building. He rapped hard and Nurse Sue raised her blinds. Her eyes opened wide as he held the manhole cover out with one arm. His bicep was the size of a softball. Uncle Nick called loudly enough for her to hear through the glass, "Wear something sexy!"

Humor is Therapeutic

Uncle Rob

During one of our summer cookouts Uncle Rob showed us how skilled he was at the game of horseshoes. At ten years of age, I had no biases that would create any doubt or concern at all. In fact, I admired Uncle Rob for his ability as a person—not a guy in a wheelchair. So it was not unusual for him to wave us on as we entered the house to eat in the comfort of air conditioning. Uncle Rob chose to stay outside and throw horseshoes. After finishing my meal I carried a plate outside for Uncle Rob, who was lying on his back in the grass—with his shirt off.

Curiously I asked, "You OK, Uncle Rob?"

Matter of factly he answered, "Yeah, I got hung up on the corner of the pit and spilled."

"Why didn't you call for help?"

"I didn't need help. Once I was down I realized I could use a tan!"

We shared a laugh as we righted his chair together. It wasn't an embarrassed laugh, or even an anxious laugh. It was a genuinely funny moment shared between an uncle and a nephew.

Disabled Does Not Mean Incompetent

Uncle Fred

My first vehicle was a used pick-up truck that I bought from a contractor, for whom I worked as a laborer. At 16, I was just happy to have a vehicle, even though it bared the scars common to construction-site trucks. One of the first people I showed my new truck was my Uncle Fred, who lived nearby. Uncle Fred wheeled around the truck and gave it a thorough inspection. He transferred easily from his chair to the front seat to start it and listen to the engine. After, he transitioned back to the chair and wheeled around to lift the hood. At this point I suspected that Uncle Fred was just going through the motions. I knew he worked on cars during his ambulatory youth, but all of this pomp and circumstance was starting to delay my next stop to show off my truck.

After about ten minutes of inspection, Uncle Fred offered his opinion that everything was fine except the body and paint.

"The only thing wrong with her is her shell. I could fix her in a weekend, you know...cheaper than any shop in town!"

Uh oh, I thought. Now I'm going to have to tell him I don't want him to work on my truck. Talking about the glory days was one thing, I thought. But messing with my truck was out of the question.

Uncle Fred must have seen the expression change on my face. His face grew serious. I think he knew what I was thinking. Before I could make up an excuse he had launched himself up into the engine compartment. He used his arms to position his legs next to the engine for leverage. With one giant punch, his open palm rammed the underside of my hood. I heard the metallic thud of sheet-metal changing shape, and sure enough, the indentation in the hood was gone. The next weekend my truck was with Uncle Fred.

Recognize the Whole Person

Uncle John

I always looked forward to visiting Uncle John. He was different than most of my uncles in that he had a wife, two children, and a single family home in the suburbs. We occasionally ate dinner while visiting. Johnny Jr. was older than I. He was in high school then, and apparently experimenting with his newfound appreciation for adolescent independence.

We were all in the living room when Johnny walked in and announced that he was going to a friend's for dinner. Uncle John looked at him sharply. "We have guests. Don't be rude." At that, Johnny started to protest, "But dad...," until Uncle John interrupted. "I said you are eating with us. End of discussion!"

Johnny clenched his jaw, and turned to walk out the door. Uncle John grabbed his cane by the rubber tip and hooked Johnny by his trailing leg. With one yank Johnny landed on the floor by Uncle John's feet.

"You can eat at the table or you can go to your room...but you will not leave this house tonight!" Johnny could have managed to get away, I thought. It was a matter of respect, not physical prowess. After this, I viewed Uncle John differently. Once I looked past his physical disability, I was able to see a father, not unlike my own in his temperament and disciplinary style.

PART I:

Adapt, Improvise and Overcome

Chapter 1: Introduction

Chapter 2: The Learner

Chapter 3: The Teacher

Chapter 4: Adapting the Environment and Task

Chapter 5: Improvising Equipment

Introduction

HOW TO USE THIS BOOK

This is not a traditional text-style book. I wrote it for a person, much like myself, who is too busy teaching to sift through texts laden with technical jargon and theoretical orientations. It is my goal to provide a book that is both practical and user-friendly. This book should be used as a recipe-style resource to which teachers may refer when planning activities for students with disabilities. In keeping with the "Whole Child" philosophy, material is included to meet the developmental needs of students with physical disabilities, as well as cognitive and affective disabilities.

Much of the material is original. It was developed and field-tested during my eight years serving as the director of physical education and athletics at the Kennedy Krieger Institute in Baltimore, Maryland. The reader should become familiar with the concepts and terminology in Part I of the book. These concepts are then incorporated into each instructional sport unit found in Part II of the book—Application.

I write as I teach—in an informal, friendly, and hopefully humorous way. One of my techniques for sharing information with the reader is to share true stories, vignettes, and case study examples of students with whom I have worked. The following is an example of how I share my experiences to convey a message or make a point.

> ### Instructional Tip 1-1
>
> **Part II of this book—Application, may be used best as a quick reference once the concepts and terminology of Part I are understood.**

 ### REAL-LIFE EXAMPLE 1-1

During one of my first student-teaching observations, I observed a class that included a student in a wheelchair. The teacher was apparently relying on the itinerant teacher to teach the student in a one-to-one capacity. An announcement over the intercom let the teacher know that the itinerant teacher was out sick today. The teacher looked at me and said, "That's just great! Now what am I supposed to do with a wheelchair kid?" I thought to myself, "That's an unusual thing for a teacher to say." The teacher thought for a moment and then whined, "The gym is no place for wheelchairs...they should have some other place to go!" Frustrated, the teacher confronted the student in the wheelchair. "Your teacher is out sick...so you'll just have to sit out and watch today." Apparently, the teacher felt better now that the "problem child" was out of the way.

After a decade specializing in teaching both able-bodied and physically disabled students in the same gym, at the same time, I can proudly say that none has ever been asked to sit out and watch. In retrospect, I believe the teacher spoke out of frustration—born of ignorance and professional incompetence. This does not excuse the behavior, but it does explain it. While many teachers are not this flagrant with their disdain for teaching students with disabilities, most will admit a level of anxiety associated with teaching students with physical disabilities. This book is for those of you who are willing, but not fully able in terms of professional skills, to incorporate students with disabilities into the "mix" of their non-disabled peers. If seeing a student who uses a wheelchair, cane, or walker enter your facility makes you the least bit anxious—this book is for you. Read. Reflect. Laugh. Learn. And by all means, put this book into practice.

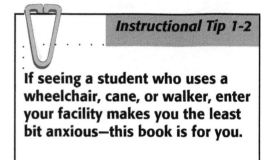

Instructional Tip 1-2

If seeing a student who uses a wheelchair, cane, or walker, enter your facility makes you the least bit anxious—this book is for you.

THE GROWING NEED

I have heard the question phrased in different ways—camouflaged with educational jargon and double-speak, but the harsh reality is that many movement professionals are asking, "Why do we have to teach *them*?" My first reaction is, if you refer to people with disabilities as *"them,"* then *"you"* are in the wrong profession. Should you honestly view people with disabilities as fundamentally different than you (assuming you are able-bodied), then your first task is to open your mind and broaden your perspective. In case you need a few reasons other than my opinion, review the following facts.

Legislation mandates that students with disabilities receive free appropriate public education. The law also requires that students be educated in the least restrictive environment. While many programs are slow to follow this legislation, the establishment of special education advocacy agencies in many districts has been catalysts for compliance. Many education officials are being held accountable for ensuring the law is followed.

This is why physical educators have seen an increase in the number of physically disabled students in their gymnasiums and on their athletic fields in the last decade. The bottom line is the factors of the law, and increased accountability to follow it, will ensure that students with special needs will be included in physical education, recreation, and athletic programs in ever increasing numbers.

A logical extension is that administrators are holding staff professionally accountable for following the law. In addition, staff are being held accountable for demonstrating outcomes for the students in their classes. Teachers who ask disabled students to "Sit out and watch," will not receive satisfactory evaluations and will jeopardize their tenure.

Besides the law and professional accountability, professionals are ethically responsible to treat students with respect and dignity. I like to think of ethical responsibility as the "Do no

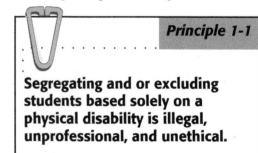

Principle 1-1

Segregating and or excluding students based solely on a physical disability is illegal, unprofessional, and unethical.

harm" principle. If you think there is no harm in excluding physically disabled students, just ask them how they feel about the situation. Segregating and or excluding students based solely on their disability is illegal, unprofessional, and unethical.

MEETING THE NEED

The new millennium brings with it a new challenge for professionals. Many who once asked, "Do we have to teach them?" are now asking, "So what do we do with them?" This is the fundamental question addressed by this book. In answering this question, Part I establishes a foundation of philosophy, principles, and concepts that will be necessary to effectively employ the strategies and techniques in Part II of this book—Application. Part I will include operational definitions, and introduces the IPI inclusion model. We will also address the primary factors that influence student success: The Learner, The Teacher, The Task, and the Environment.

PHILOSOPHY

I have never wasted my time engaging in academic debates over the effectiveness of inclusion. I am neither a supporter nor an opponent, as I believe the efficacy of inclusion depends on a variety of factors that vary from school to school. As the director of physical education for a non-public special education facility, I was tasked with providing meaningful physical education experiences for a wide range of students in any given class—all of whom had various special education needs. At one point I was teaching 21 different classes—most of which were grouped by considering a combination of cognitive and behavioral factors. "Physical disability" was never a factor in determining class groupings. With respect to physical abilities and

Principle 1-2

Students may be grouped according to their Cognitive (Thinking), Affective (behavior and emotional stability), or Psychomotor (Movement) development. The fundamental question is which grouping will facilitate learning most effectively for a given discipline.

disabilities, I developed professionally in a fully inclusive setting. That is, most of my classes contained students who were both physically able and physically disabled.

I learned to appreciate the benefits of having students with a wide range of physical abilities in my classes. In fact, given the choice I would give cognitive abilities the priority for class groupings, followed by behavior and affect, and lastly physical abilities.

I challenge the notion that students need to be grouped according to physical ability for meaningful learning to occur. I have demonstrated that effective psychomotor development can occur when students are grouped by cognitive abilities. In other words, the students in my classes are more alike in reading, writing, and math than they are in their physical abilities. This is why I have ambulatory students in the same class as students who use wheelchairs, canes, and walkers. Students are grouped into classes for a variety of reasons. Whether the students are clustered by the administration by cognitive abilities, like in my case, or, are clustered by course election, as in secondary settings, movement professionals are more likely than ever to see students using wheelchairs, canes, and walkers in their programs.

I also challenge the belief that "Special Educators" need to be brought in (itinerant teachers) to teach students with physical disabilities. Teachers who understand motor development and teaching pedagogy should be able to individualize instruction for all students. I dislike the separation that exists between special educators and regular educators—especially in physical education. I maintain that good teachers should be able to individualize instruction—which is what special educators do by definition. Since the two disciplines of regular education and special education co-exist in most settings, the two should work together in a collaborative way. Special educators should work with regular educators with the goal of including students with physical disabilities with their non-disabled peers—not providing separate "pull-out" service.

I defend my position by example. I was trained as a regular physical educator in a four-year program that included one course in Adapted Physical Education. I was fortunate to be hired by a newly developing non-public pro-

Principle 1-3

Regarding the discipline of Physical Education, special educators should work collaboratively with regular educators with the goal of including students with physical disabilities with their non-disabled peers—not providing separate "pull-out" service.

gram, serving students with special needs. I designed the physical education program without any additional special education training. I simply employed sound teaching methods and individualized instruction. I worked closely with special educators who had expertise with specific disabilities—inviting them to co-teach with me in the gymnasium. In five years we built a program that earned National Recognition as a featured part of our Blue Ribbon School Honors. In my seventh year I was named National Teacher of the Year by the National Association of Private Schools for Exceptional Children—a special education organization!

CHAPTER 2

The Learner

People often think of Adapted Physical Education and Recreation instruction as it relates to students with physical challenges. Since these are the disabilities that are visible to the observer, it may appear that instructional adaptations are limited to addressing students' physical needs. In fact, more Adaptation to the educational environment, and Improvisation of equipment is required for the disabilities that are not noticeable to the untrained observer. This section identifies the Federal Handicapping Conditions recognized by federal law as it applies to providing students a Free Appropriate Public Education in the Least Restrictive Environment. Also included is a description of three degrees of disabilities, and an overview of the educational domains that form the foundation of the "Whole Child" philosophy.

FEDERAL HANDICAPPING CONDITIONS

The following conditions are recognized nationally and documented as one or more disabilities, required by law, to be addressed in accordance with the student's Individualized Education Plan (IEP).

Orthopedically Impaired (OI). Federal Handicapping Code (FHC) (07). This includes disabilities related to the musculo-skeletal system that impede developmentally appropriate movement.

Traumatically Brain Injured (TBI). FHC (13). This includes physical, cognitive, and socio-emotional disabilities related to brain damage resulting from a traumatic injury.

Multi-disabled (MD). FHC (10). This includes the net effect of two or more disabilities that affect developmentally appropriate function and performance. Many students with the multiple disabilities diagnosis have a combined learning disability and emotional disability. It is also common for sensory impairment to be one of the conditions of the multiply disabled.

Learning Disabled (LD). FHC (09). This includes students with a significant discrepancy between their academic ability and performance, as determined by standardized test scores. Learning disabilities include the common diagnosis of Attention Deficit and or Hyperactivity Disorder (ADHD). Students with learning disabilities typically score below their peers of the same age in reading, writing, and or mathematics. Often times there are associated difficulties with speech and language processing, which makes understanding and following staff directions challenging. These students typically have associated behavioral difficulties in the school setting. Students with learning disabilities are frequently prescribed medications to help them concentrate, focus, and or control hyperactivity.

Emotionally Disturbed (ED). FHC (06). This includes students with a variety of challenges regarding feelings and emotions. Some have difficulty managing anger, expressing grief, accepting authority, and/or getting along with others. Often times students with emotional disturbance have histories of depression. During adolescence, students with emotional disturbance are particularly at risk for abusing drugs and alcohol. Students with emotional disabilities are frequently prescribed medications to help them cope with daily life.

Visually Impaired (VI). FHC (05). This includes a wide spectrum of visual disabilities ranging from those that are correctable with prescription lenses, to those that are not correctable. Not all students who wear glasses are diagnosed as visually impaired; however, if prescription lenses are recommended by an optometrist, then the student is recognized as having a special learning need.

Hearing Impaired (HI). FHC (02). Like VI, this includes hearing disabilities ranging from those that require hearing devices to those that are not correctable. As with glasses and contact lenses, any physician-recommended device needs to be considered required for optimal performance in movement programs.

Other Health Impaired (OHI). FHC (08). This includes diseases, conditions, and allergies that inhibit developmentally appropriate function and performance. Common examples include asthma, diabetes, seizure disorders, and allergies.

Autism [Pervasive Developmental Disability]. (PDD) (14). There is a wide spectrum of degrees and types of Autism, which literally means, non-relating. People with Autism typically have difficulties with verbal and non-verbal communication, social interactions, and leisure or play activities. They may demonstrate repeated body movements like hand flapping or rocking, unusual attachments to objects, and they commonly resist changes in daily routines.

DEGREE OF DISABILITY

Disabilities may be grouped into categories based on the extent of the disability. The American Psychiatric Association defines cognitive categories, or degrees, as either mild, moderate, severe, or profound. The clinical determination of degree of cognitive disability is a function of a person's IQ scores. To the physical educator or recreation instructor, the line that distinguishes one degree from the other is not always clearly delineated. Physical disabilities are presented for the purposes of this book as either mild, moderate, or severe, with respect to overall motor performance and the ability to be meaningfully included in movement activities. The following case study examples will help the teacher or instructor to recognize a student's degree of disability as it relates to participation in physical education and recreation activities.

Mild Disabilities
Definition: This intensity includes disabilities that are least limiting in terms of developmental functioning and physical performance. Students with mild cognitive, emotional, or physical disabilities are sometimes not apparent to the untrained observer. Students with mild orthopedic impairments usually do not require wheelchairs, canes, or walkers. They may, however, use braces, and/or orthopedic devices to facilitate safe, comfortable, and efficient movement.

The following case study examples illustrate how students with mild disabilities may present themselves in a physical education or recreation environment.

Case Study Examples: Mild Disabilities

Josh—Orthopedic Impairment (OI). Josh has Kyphosis, an unnatural hunch-like curvature of the upper back and spine. Josh is self-conscious of his condition and wears sweatshirts during physical education. He tires easily when tasked with upper-body activities, and has limited shoulder flexibility. Overhand throwing is awkward for Josh.

Liz—Traumatic Brain Injury (TBI). Liz is a first grade student who was involved in an automobile collision at age four which required brain surgery. She was thrown from her car seat, which was improperly fastened. Two years following the trauma, her motor function nearly matches that of her peers. Liz has difficulty maintaining balance and struggles with activities that require agility. She likes to play tag, but frequently trips or falls while running.
*Liz is featured in each of the sports chapters in Part II—Application of this book.

Terrell—Multidisabled (MD). Terrell has Cerebral Palsy (CP) which affects his left foot and leg, and is diagnosed as having Attention-Deficit-Hyperactive-Disorder. Terrell's CP is mild, and he sometimes chooses to use a walker when an activity requires agility and speed. Terrell cannot keep up with his peers during activities involving running. It is difficult to keep Terrell focused. He works for five minutes, then loses interest and begins off-task behaviors.

Jerome—Visually Impaired (VI). Jerome wears thick eye glasses to correct his vision. During physical education, Jerome wears a rubber strap to keep his glasses secure. Without his glasses, Jerome would not be able to participate safely.

Leverne—Hearing Impaired (HI). Leverne wears a hearing amplification device, called an auditory trainer, in each ear. He also wears a receiver that is wired to the ear pieces. The teacher wears a transmitter and speaks into a small microphone that clips to the shirt collar. Without the device, Leverne cannot hear the teacher's directions.

Lisa—Other Health Impaired (OHI). Lisa is allergic to Latex. If Latex products are in the same room as Lisa, her skin develops red itchy patches. The worst reaction she had was in physical education when her teacher used Latex balloons during a volleyball lesson.

Moderate Disabilities

Definition: This intensity includes disabilities that are moderately limiting in terms of developmental functioning. Students with moderate disabilities commonly use walkers, canes, and in some cases, wheelchairs. They may also wear corrective equipment, like ankle braces, and protective equipment, like helmets and padding. Some students may also be considered medically fragile due to specific conditions. This would include students with Spina Bifida who have implanted shunts in their brains, or students with heart conditions that need to limit aerobic intensity.

Case Study Examples: Moderate Disabilities

Phil—Orthopedic Impairment (OI). Phil was born with a severely deformed right foot. Complications with his condition required amputation below the knee. Phil used a wheelchair as a child, and was independent and competitive in athletics. At age 17, he is learning how to use his new prosthetic limb to help him participate on foot. He switches between his wheelchair and his prosthesis during 11th grade physical education, depending on the activity and his confidence level.
*Phil is featured in each of the sports chapters in Part II—Application of this book.

Jason—Traumatic Brain Injury (TBI). Jason was struck by a moving automobile while riding his bicycle. He sustained brain damage and required surgery. He has a surgically implanted shunt at the base of his skull that prevents the potential build-up of fluid around his brain. Jason walks with a quad cane and is willing to participate in any activity—except those that require rolling or becoming inverted. The feeling of vertigo associated with rolling or spinning that exhilarates many students, creates fear and panic for Jason. Jason wears a lacrosse helmet while participating in sports with a moving ball or object that may strike him in the head. He can walk quickly, but is not able to run.

Maggie—(MD). Maggie is a seventh grade student who was born with Cerebral Palsy, and uses a wheelchair for most daily activities. Her paralysis is limited to her legs, and she compensates well with her upper body. Using her arm strength, Maggie can transition into and out of her chair independently. She also uses a walker for activities that do not involve both hands. Maggie is energetic, friendly, and ambitious. She enjoys challenging her able-bodied peers in competition, and frequently wins. Maggie also has a learning disability, and reads five years below that of her peers.

*Maggie is featured in each of the sports chapters in Part II—Application of this book.

Lynn—Visually Impaired (VI). Lynn is legally blind. She is able to differentiate between light and dark, and can interpret shapes from a close distance. Lynn has developed an acute sense of hearing, and uses her ears to compensate for her visual disability. Lynn can catch most balls with the sound made by a bounce pass.

Michael—Hearing Impaired (HI). Michael was born deaf. He has learned to talk with basic words, but is difficult to understand. He is much better at communicating with sign language. Michael is one of the most skilled athletes in the school.

William—Other Health Impaired (OHI). William has a seizure disorder and severe asthma. William carries an inhaler with him during physical education class and is permitted to use it at his discretion. William has mild seizures which, to an observer, appear that he is staring blankly. Once during the school day, William had a major seizure in which he fell to the floor and shook with full body spasms for two minutes.

Severe Disabilities

Definition: This intensity includes disabilities that are severely limiting in terms of developmental functioning and performance. Students with severe and profound disabilities often require electric wheelchairs that are operated by hand, arm, head, or breath. The wheelchair is used for transportation, as well as postural support.

Case Study Examples: Severe Disabilities

Kevin—Orthopedically Impaired (OI). Kevin is a fourth grade student who broke his neck diving into a swimming pool and striking the bottom with his head. Kevin is paralyzed from his neck down, with very minimal voluntary movement initiated by his left wrist. This is the movement that he is learning to control in an effort to manipulate the joystick of his wheelchair. Kevin requires two adults to transition him into and out of his wheelchair. Once unstrapped, Kevin is dependent on staff for all manipulation and positioning of his body.

*Kevin is featured in each of the sports chapters in Part II—Application of this book.

EDUCATIONAL DOMAINS

This book approaches adapting and improvising sport and recreational activities for the Whole Person—including thoughts, feelings, senses, and movement abilities. Respectively, these are referred to as the cognitive (thinking), affective (feeling), sensorimotor (sensing), and psychomotor (physical movement) domains.

The following examples illustrate how adapting or improvising may facilitate student success with respect to the educational domains.

The Cognitive Domain

As I entered my first teaching position, a physical education teacher in a non-public special education facility, I was particularly confident in my ability to teach the "whole child." After all, I had just completed a four-year program of study and a student-teaching internship. It was during my first week of teaching that I realized how much I did not know about students with special learning needs—particularly how to communicate effectively with students who have learning disabilities.

Real Life Example 2-1
The Cognitive Domain

There was one particular class, during my first year of teaching, that never seemed to follow the class routine of sitting at the chalkboard for review and closure—a routine known as "summary." Class after class, I lectured and explained about our "summary" routine. Nonetheless, when the end of class arrived they still acted as if they did not know what to do. One day, before class started I asked the students to tell their teacher what we would do at the chalkboard at the end of class. Not one hand was raised. The students looked at each other blankly. I repeated the word slowly and deliberately..."summmarrrry." Then I asked the class to repeat it, and they did—several times. I looked at the teacher proudly for affirmation of a job well done. She then asked the class, "What is a summary?" After a few moments, Timothy raised his hand and started to sing, "Summary...makes me feel fine..." (If you don't get the joke, he was alluding to the 70s pop music classic, "Summer Breeze.")

In the years to follow I learned to understand and appreciate the cognitive challenges of our students. The key to developing appropriate lessons is understanding students' realities and the characteristics of their disabilities. Once I began teaching students instead of teaching lessons, I was more successful.

I now know I was ineffective teaching the students about our "summary" routine because I used verbal directions to communicate to students with auditory processing difficulties. I learned something called the VAKT approach to teaching—Visual, Auditory, Kinesthetic, and Tactile. In short, students learn best when they have the opportunity to practice via sight, sound, movement, and touch.

Principle 2-1

It is more effective to teach students than to teach lessons. Start by understanding the nature of students' disabilities, then individualize your instruction to meet their needs.

Example of Cognitive Adaptations

I initially had a problem getting students to use the proper hand placement on a variety of sticks and equipment. Few students responded to verbal directions, and most forgot shortly after I demonstrated the correct technique for them. That is when I learned the power of color coding.

All sticks in our program requiring two-hand grips use the same color coding to help students remember proper hand placement. Our rule is, "Dominant hand on the blue tape and non-dominant hand on the yellow tape." In student-friendly terms they are the "strong" hand and the "weak" hand. Whether using a hockey stick or a lacrosse stick, students universally understand the teaching cue, "Strong hand on Blue."

The Affective Domain

Unfortunately, adapting activities to accommodate students' emotional needs is not a common practice in many programs. For many students, physical activities are a source of anxiety and frustration. In my experiences, these adaptations have the most implications for fostering positive student attitudes and limiting inappropriate acting-out behaviors.

Example of Affective Adaptations

One of the most anxiety-producing events for students is to "strike out" in front of their peers during softball or baseball. To alleviate the stress, develop a standard policy that students may not strike out in the game. Once two strikes are earned from pitched balls, the student will then need to toss the ball to him or herself while batting. Once two strikes are earned this way, the student will need to strike the ball from a tee or a cone. The student may swing as many times as required to hit the ball. This technique is effective for students from elementary school to high school. I include it in this example because it has been one of the best received adaptations in our program.

The Psychomotor Domain

The Psychomotor Domain relates to the physical aspects of students' development. It includes development of locomotor (running, hopping, skipping...), manipulative (throwing, catching, striking...), and stability (balancing, hanging, swinging...) skills. Students may develop these fundamental skills into sport and recreation skills as they grow and mature. The psychomotor domain also includes the development of skills in physical fitness, rhythms and dance, and gymnastics.

Real Life Example 2-2
The Psychomotor Domain

I was somewhat unprepared for working with Paul, a ten-year-old student with Cerebral Palsy paralyzing all four limbs. Paul was also legally blind, hearing impaired, and very limited intellectually. My principal was empathetic and provided me with some in-service training time to learn how to best work with Paul. I visited several programs and observed Adapted Physical Educators working with students much like Paul. In no time I had put together a sensory-stimulation program designed to meet Paul's physical needs. The primary theme for our work was "vestibular and tactile stimulation." Our activities looked more like wrestling than physical education. I flexed and extended his joints, rubbed and massaged his muscles, and contorted him into as many positions as his body would allow. All the while, I kept reminding Paul that we are doing all of this to "Stimulate his muscles!" As we worked, I would repeat, "Stimulate, Stimulate, Stimulate!" The more I said it, the more Paul laughed. It became an ongoing joke between us. One day during our usual rough-and-tumble activities, I inadvertently pulled Paul's sweat pants down over his bottom. I pulled them back without missing a beat and continued the muscle work. Following class, our principal stopped in to observe Paul's progress. I then asked Paul to explain to the principal what we did in class. Paul was in a particularly silly mood, and answered while choking back his laughter, "Mr. Williams pulled down my pants...and he stimulated me!"

All I could think about was all of the time and energy that I spent developing a specialized physical program...and this was the "thanks" I received. My principal was understanding.

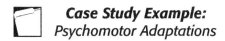

Case Study Example:
Psychomotor Adaptations

Terrell
Terrell becomes easily frustrated when playing volleyball. He is not developmentally ready to return a volleyball in flight from across the net. He is able to "set" a volleyball if the teacher tosses it softly to him, but not if it is moving too fast. During the volleyball game Terrell chooses to be a pass player, which means he can play a ball that is caught by a teammate, and tossed to him. Terrell prefers this option instead of playing in a modified game with a beach ball.

The Sensorimotor Domain
The sensorimotor domain involves the integration of vision, hearing, and touch with the muscular and nervous system. A common phrase related to the sensorimotor domain is "eye-hand coordination." Students with sensory impairments typically have significant difficulties with movement activities.

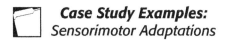

Case Study Examples:
Sensorimotor Adaptations

Lynn
Consider including Lynn (legally blind) in a relay race during track and field. Lynn's path will be defined by a taut cord, threaded through a ten-inch hollow aluminum baton, running from the start to the finish. Lynn will run while holding onto the baton as it glides along the cord. Several knots at the end signal Lynn to come to a stop.

Josh
Josh has difficulty coordinating both hands during the underhand badminton serve. Every time Josh drops the shuttle with an outstretched left arm, he extends his right elbow too far and the head of the racquet misses the shuttle. After presenting several options to Josh, he decides to use the "Launch" technique. This involves balancing the shuttle, feathers down, on the face of the racquet. The racquet is then flung forward, launching the shuttle up and over the net. By adapting the task requirement, this technique limits the eye-hand coordination needed to be successful.

CHAPTER 3

The Teacher

The physical education or recreation teacher of students with special needs must have expertise in both content and process. Content expertise relates to an understanding of motor development, instructional pedagogy, curriculum development, lesson planning, and assessment. Staff should also be familiar with the safe and ethical practices that are standard within the movement profession. Process expertise relates to therapeutic behavior management, motivating learners, developing structure, and working collaboratively with others. While these topics are beyond the scope of this book, they are nevertheless critical to effective teaching. It is assumed that readers of this book have a basic background in instructional content and process.

This section introduces the IPI model, and the cycle of change that is likely to result as a function of including wheelchairs, canes, and walkers in your program.

IPI INCLUSION MODEL

The Individual, Preparatory, Inclusive (IPI) inclusion model provides a progressive framework for teaching students with special needs and physical disabilities when they are grouped in the same class with their non-disabled peers. At any given point in a lesson, students with special needs should be engaged in one of the three levels of participation. Students without

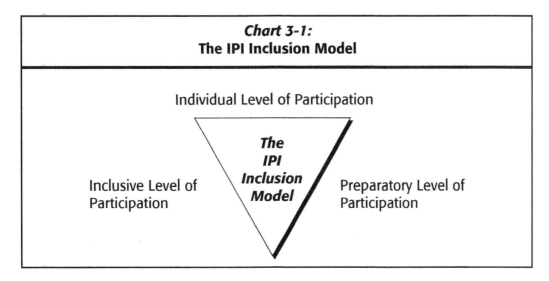

Chart 3-1:
The IPI Inclusion Model

Individual Level of Participation

The IPI Inclusion Model

Inclusive Level of Participation

Preparatory Level of Participation

disabilities who are the majority of the class, and are engaged in non-adaptive activities, are referred to as the main body of the class.

Individual Level

Definition: This level provides a meaningful activity related to the objectives of the lesson that can be demonstrated individually with either direct teacher support, or indirect teacher support.

Purpose: There are several purposes of individual participation. The first is that it affords students the opportunity to experience success in a non-threatening environment. The second is that it provides the student the opportunity to become familiar with specialized equipment that may not be appropriate for participation with non-disabled peers. The third is that it allows the student to remain on task while the teacher addresses the needs of the main body of the class. As a rule, individual work should not exceed ⅓ of class time. It is a necessary logistical component, but should not become the focus of participation for students with special needs. This would be segregation, and not an acceptable practice.

Procedure: Part II of this book will address a variety of individualized activities specific to units of instruction. The teacher sets up a station where a student may participate individually, or with a peer assistant. When the class arrives, the teacher gives directions to the main body of the class to get them started. The teacher then gives directions to the student at the individual station. At various points in the lesson the student may transition into preparatory or inclusive activities and back to the individual station.

Case Study Example:
Individual Level

Volleyball. Lesson 1 of 8 lessons total. Maggie is asked to stretch her arms with Gina, a senior who was trained as a peer assistant for physical education. Meanwhile, the teacher directs the students to begin serving warm-ups with partners. The teacher then directs Maggie to position her chair under the basketball goal and asks Maggie to hold onto one end of the tether cord. The tether cord loops over the basketball rim like a pulley such that the ball is suspended one foot from the floor. Maggie then manipulates the cord to raise or lower the ball until it swings up and over a four-foot-high net.

This activity is included at the individual level, and may not help Maggie become included in the volleyball game with her peers. It does, however, provide a volleyball-related activity that challenges Maggie at her developmental ability. It also affords the teacher time to structure a preparatory and or inclusive activity for Maggie.

Preparatory Level

Definition: This level provides realistic "practice" that focuses on a skill that will be used by the student when he or she is included with the main body of the class. This "practice" can be demonstrated individually with either direct teacher support, or indirect teacher support.

Purpose: Preparatory activities "prepare" the student for the physical, cognitive, and social demands of the inclusive activity. It is overwhelming for the student with special needs to be incorporated into an unfamiliar game. The preparatory activity provides an opportunity for a developmentally appropriate task, or piece of the bigger game, to be practiced and refined in the safe, controlled setting. When the student is integrated into the main body of the class, he or she will approach the task with greater competence and confidence, having practiced it repeatedly.

Procedure: Part II of this book will address a variety of preparatory activities specific to units of instruction. The teacher identifies a specific game-related skill that the student is developmentally able to master in a few lessons. The skill should be closely related to a skill that is associated with the game that the main body of the class is playing. The skill should also be one that is likely to be accepted by the main body of the class—that is, it will not slow down the pace and or quality of the game. Once the student masters the skill in a static environment, the teacher includes a few trained peers to make a small group lead-up activity. This allows the student to experience a dynamic play environment and the pressure associated with competition. The teacher then sets up a small preparatory game including the basic rules, terms, and scoring procedures. Once the student demonstrates proficiency, he or she is ready to be included in the main body of the class.

Case Study Example:
Preparatory Level

Volleyball. Lessons 2, 3, and 4 of 8 lessons total. Maggie (grade 7) expresses interest in playing in a volleyball game with the main body of the class on the first day of the unit. After a basic skills test, the teacher learns that Maggie cannot serve, set, or bump the volleyball over the regulation net from her wheelchair. The teacher also learns that Maggie does not know many of the rules, or how to keep score. The preparatory skill that the teacher identifies is called the "catch-underhand-serve" skill. This skill involves Maggie catching a regulation volleyball as it is tossed over a five-foot high net. Then Maggie holds the ball in her left palm, swings her right arm back with an underhand motion, and then forward to strike the ball from her palm. When Maggie is able to demonstrate the catch-underhand-serve over the net three out of five times, the teacher invites three classmates over for a small group game. During lessons 2, 3, and 4 Maggie practices with various small groups, preparing for the game with the main body of the class.

Inclusive Level

Definition: This level provides realistic "game-play," incorporating a skill that was mastered at the preparatory level of participation.

Purpose: The purpose of the inclusive activity is to provide the opportunity for the student to demonstrate a newly mastered adaptive skill in a competitive game with the main body of the class.

Procedure: Part II of this book will address a variety of inclusive activities specific to units of instruction. The teacher selects a group of students from the main body of the class, and explains the adaptive skill that the "included" student will use to participate. The teacher should demonstrate the nature of the skill by role-playing for the group during simulated game-play. The main body of the class should have the opportunity to ask questions and make comments. Some initial resistance from a select few students is expected, and easily countered with positive responses from the teacher. The teacher should be actively engaged in the beginning of the activity until the "included" student demonstrates success. Consistent praise and constructive feedback is necessary to keep the group on task and positive.

Case Study Example:
Inclusive Level

Volleyball. Lessons 5, 6, 7, of 8 lessons total. Maggie (grade 7) is excited because today she gets to try out her newly acquired "catch-underhand-serve skill" in a "real" volleyball game with her peers. The teacher asks Maggie to practice the "catch-underhand-serve skill" with Gina, a peer assistant, while the main body of the class forms groups and begins game-play. The teacher then demonstrates the adaptive skill that Maggie will use during the game. The teacher sits in a wheelchair and demonstrates exactly how Maggie will participate. Then Maggie demonstrates her "catch-underhand-serve" skill for the class. It is agreed that Maggie can safely catch any ball that reaches her on a bounce. Maggie asks that the player next to her catch any ball that may hit her during flight. Any student on Maggie's team may catch the ball, as long as they bounce pass it to Maggie. Maggie may choose to pass the ball to a teammate, or "serve" it over the net in place of a traditional "set" or "bump" return. Maggie played one whole game and held the ball six times. She passed to teammates twice and returned the ball over the net successfully three times. This is about the same success rate her peers had returning the volleyball over the net. After the game, the teacher encourages Maggie to work on a different preparatory skill in next class—the "toss and set." Maggie is optimistic that she would master that, too, and try it in her next "inclusive" game.

PROGRESSIVE-COMPETITIVE-LEVELS STRATEGY

Teachers of physical education and recreation spend a great deal of time during their professional preparation learning to task-analyze sports—breaking the activities into basic skill components. Unfortunately, few professionals implement these skills effectively once they begin working with students. Elementary teachers historically teach sports and activities in a progressive developmental way. I believe this is because the variation of student growth and development is very noticeable in elementary school. For example, third grade students do not usually play a regulation game of volleyball, tennis, or basketball. Instead, the teachers provide a variety of lead-up activities and adapted variations of the "official" sport.

As students age, they are expected to have developed specific sports competencies. One of the basic principles of motor development is that sports skills competencies are age related, not age dependent. Yet students in the intermediate and secondary grades are constantly put into anxiety-producing situations where they are forced to execute skills that they have not mastered.

One of the key elements of developing success-oriented activities for students is to implement the Progressive-Competitive-Levels (PCL) strategy. PCL is simply presenting any

> ### Principle 3-1
>
> **Sports-skills competencies are age related, not age dependent. It is not acceptable to expect all students to participate at the highest level of performance because of their age or size.**

sport or activity as a series of levels—each progressively more challenging than the last. The highest level of play should be regulation game-play. Part II will include Progressive-Competitive-Levels for each sport or activity. Below is an example of 7 Level Volleyball, which is the most popular PCL sequence in our program. It is liked by students, as well as staff. During my ten years of teaching physical education, I have never observed an entire class that was ready to play level 7 volleyball—regular education or special education! The most skilled classes make it to level 5, with a few students opting to play at levels 6 and 7. This is a powerful concept. I would not teach without it.

Progressive-Competitive-Levels Example:
7-Level Volleyball

Description: Students are arranged in standard volleyball formation, on either a standard or modified court. The equipment, including the net and ball, can be improvised or regulation, such that student success is maximized. The adaptations that follow involve modifications of the required skills (task), and both the court area and rules (environment). Students who are expected to participate in competitive volleyball activities should begin by playing level 1 Volleyball. Once the majority of the students in the group have demonstrated mastery at level 1, they should be allowed to transition to level 2 play.

Students who have not mastered the skills for a particular level should be allowed to continue playing at their respective level while the remainder of the group moves to the next difficulty level. It is common to have students playing at different levels in the same game. For example, in any given game Terrell is allowed to catch the ball on one bounce, while Maggie may only catch the ball in the air. The remainder of the players may not be allowed to catch the ball at all.

Students may demonstrate mastery of level 1 or level 2 skills in a few minutes. The teacher should allow the students to progress when they demonstrate readiness, or the students will become frustrated and lose interest. In my experience, most intermediate classes progress through levels 1 and 2 in the introductory lesson. Most will progress through levels 3 and 4 during the second lesson. Ultimately, the majority of the students will reach their competitive limit at levels 4 or 5. By the conclusion of a volleyball unit, a select few students play at levels 1, 2, or 3. The majority of the students play at levels 4 or 5, while some advanced players compete at levels 6 or 7. If the teacher develops the criteria for progressive levels appropriately, student performance should fit the standard bell curve parameters.

Level 1: Bounce-Catch Volleyball

1. The ball is put into play with a toss or throw from the right side of the court.
2. The server may position him or herself any distance from the net to get the ball over.
3. The receiving team may catch the ball on one bounce, or in the air. Only three players are allowed to touch the ball before the ball is returned over the net.
4. The ball may bounce once when it is passed between players on the same team.
5. The ball may be returned over the net with a toss or a strike.
6. Following a side-out, the team earning the serve rotates players as usual.
7. Game-play continues until:
   A) time expires
   B) a predetermined score is reached
   C) the majority of the students demonstrate readiness to move to the next difficulty level.

Level 2: Catch Volleyball

1. All rules for level 1 apply, except:
2. Players may not let the ball bounce during the course of game-play.
3. Players may catch the ball or strike the ball during game-play.

Level 3: Serve Volleyball

1. All rules for level 2 apply except:
2. The volleyball must be put into play using the underhand serve technique.
3. The server may choose to serve from one of three positions—at the net, at mid-court, or at the baseline (regulation).

Level 4: Set Volleyball

1. All rules for level 3 apply except:
2. The ball may not be tossed over the net.
3. Players may catch a ball that is returned over the net, however the player that chooses to send it over the net must demonstrate a regulation "set" or strike.
4. The player that chooses to strike the ball may toss the ball to him or herself to execute the "set" or strike.

Level 5: Bump Volleyball

1. All rules for level 4 apply except:
2. The receiving team may not catch the ball as it is served or returned over the net.

3. The first and last touch when playing a ball must be a "set," "bump," or regulation strike.
4. A player on the receiving team may "bump" or "set" the ball to a teammate whom may catch the ball. This provides a safety net for the players with limited striking control.
5. The ball must be "set" or "bumped" over the net to resume game-play.

Level 6: Bump-Set Volleyball
1. All rules for level 5 apply except:
2. The ball may not be caught at any time during game-play.
3. Players may return the ball over the net with any strike technique.

Level 7: Regulation (Bump-Set-Spike) Volleyball
1. Regulation game-play.
2. Players are encouraged to demonstrate the bump-set-spike combination during game-play.

THE CYCLE OF CHANGE MODEL

The cycle of change refers to the predictable pattern that occurs when different routines and alternative ideas are presented to students. There will likely be initial resistance to give the new way a try. Following the Initial Resistance there will be cautious acceptance. Ultimately students will reach genuine acceptance of change.

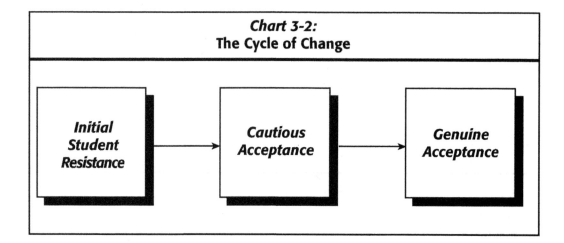

Chart 3-2:
The Cycle of Change

Initial Student Resistance → Cautious Acceptance → Genuine Acceptance

Working Through Student Resistance
The main factor that determines how the new concepts are received by students is the manner in which they are presented by the staff. All staff members need to be consistent and positive when communicating rules and procedures. A second factor is to allow students to make choices regarding their participation. For example, a student says, "Why does Josh get to serve the easy way?" An appropriate response would be, "It is an easier way, and anyone can choose to use that technique." Lastly, students will inevitably challenge the new rules. Staff needs to be prepared to set limits and provide choices. The student who refuses to bat from a tee because that is "the baby way," should hear, "You can hit from the tee or you can give your turn to a teammate, but no one gets a pitch after two strikes."

Again, the key to limiting student resistance to these alternative concepts is positive presentation by the staff. If the students do not to buy into the alternative rules, it is because the staff has failed to sell them.

Principle 3-2

Students do not fail at buying into alternative rules . . . staff fail to sell them effectively to the students. It only takes one condescending remark or gesture by staff to undermine the therapeutic intent.

CHAPTER 4

Adapting the Environment and Task

ENVIRONMENTAL FACTORS

Dynamic Play Environment

A dynamic environment requires the student to react to constantly changing variables of time and space. Anytime a competitor is involved and applying offensive or defensive pressure, the environment is dynamic. Dynamic environments are associated with goal-oriented sports such as basketball, hockey, soccer, and lacrosse.

The Static Play Environment

A static environment does not change prior to the initiation of movement by the student. The student decides when to initiate movement, and is not affected by outside influences such as defenders. Static environments are associated with sports such as golf, archery, gymnastics, and bowling. Many dynamic sports include components that are static. Consider the foul shot in basketball, the penalty kick in soccer, or the serve in tennis. Since many sports and recreational activities are combinations of dynamic and static environments, it is helpful to further define the components of these activities as either open skills or closed skills.

TASK FACTORS

Open-Skill Tasks

Open skills are demonstrated in the dynamic context. They require students to react in response to outside influences. Dribbling a basketball past a defender is an example of an open skill. So too, is batting a pitched baseball, returning a tennis serve, or catching a frisbee. Open skills are more difficult to demonstrate than closed skills and should be introduced following closed-skill practice of the same skill.

Closed-Skill Tasks

Closed skills are demonstrated in the static context. They afford the student the opportunity to decide when to initiate, perform, and follow through with a task. Throwing and jumping events in track and field activities are considered closed skills. Other examples include putting in golf and kicking off in football.

Note that sport and recreation skills may be modified by changing the environmental dynamics and the demands of the task. Changing the environmental and task variables is the fundamental key to creating developmentally appropriate activities that match student abilities. Consider the batting tee for beginning baseball players. The tee supports the ball in a static environment, which increases batting success.

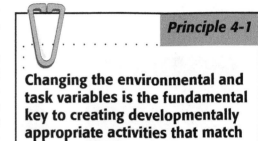

Principle 4-1

Changing the environmental and task variables is the fundamental key to creating developmentally appropriate activities that match student abilities.

When the student is ready for a greater challenge, the ball may be suspended by a tether cord to add the challenge of visually tracking and coordinating the eyes and the muscles required for batting. The progression may then include self-tossing the ball, hitting an underhand toss, and finally an overhand throw.

The following adaptations modify the task and the environment to facilitate student success. These adaptations form the foundation for including students with disabilities in competitive activities.

If teachers are going to use this book effectively, they need to think in non-traditional ways—some would call this thinking "outside the box." The three primary competitive adaptations used when working with physically disabled students in physical education include modifications to objects, space, and time. In student-friendly terms, these concepts are called hot, crease, and clock. Students would then elect the adaptation of their choice by requesting to use a hot object, be a crease player, or a clock player.

PRIMARY COMPETITIVE ADAPTATIONS (PCAS)

Definition: Any object (a ball in this example) in class that is limited to use by one player with special needs. A red Nerf ball, for example, may be designated as a hot ball for Terrell. There may be more than one hot ball in class, one designated for each student with special needs. Each hot ball needs to be different from the others, as well as distinct from the balls that the class uses. Terrell's hot ball may be orange. The majority of the class uses green Nerf balls, which are easily distinguishable from Terrell's hot ball.

Purpose: The hot ball decreases student anxiety by making a dynamic play environment static. Consider a game where there are many Nerf balls on the floor and students are dribbling with their feet. Without a hot ball, the student using a walker would likely lose his or her ball to other able-bodied classmates. During game-play the hot ball decreases student anxiety about defenders capturing it. During individual practice with multiple balls in the activity, the hot ball eliminates the anxiety associated with losing the ball to another student due to the extra time of transitioning to retrieve it.

Instructional Tip 4-1

Often times, physically disabled students do not need a hot ball (or any other adaptation). In many cases, students without physical disabilities who are less skilled and emotionally fragile, will elect this option. It is a powerful resource for students that are less skilled than the majority. Any adaptation used in this book should be made available to any student who may benefit.

Hot Concept

Procedure: During the lesson, only Terrell may touch his hot ball. The hot ball may be used for individual work, as well as during game play.

Example: **Individual work.**

The lesson involves ten students on each side of the indoor soccer area. The goal of the activity is to kick nerf balls across the centerline to the opposing team. Without a hot ball, Terrell is not likely to transition his walker to an available ball because his classmates reach them quicker. The hot ball provides a ball used exclusively by Terrell, at his individual ability level.

Case Study Example:
Terrell Hot Ball Player

During a soccer game, one green ball is designated the official ball used by the main body of the class. Terrell elects to use a hot ball because he seldom maneuvers his walker well enough to reach the game ball. Terrell plays at his own pace with his hot ball in the middle of his classmates' game-play. Terrell dribbles the ball toward the opposing team's goal. Terrell may shoot at an undefended goal, at a goal defended by a teacher, or at a goal defended by a trained peer who understands his abilities. Terrell is thrilled to be in the mix of game-play action, without the anxiety associated with defenders capturing his ball. His classmates appreciate the opportunity to include Terrell, and do not mind playing around him.

CREASE Concept

Definition: The crease (a term borrowed from Lacrosse) is a space created by the teacher and designated with clear boundaries that is limited to use by one player with special needs. In the gymnasium or outdoor court the crease may be a lane, a zone, or a position outlined by lines or cones. On the athletic field it may be designated by field chalk, painted lines, or cones.

Purpose: The purpose of the crease is to create a safe space for students with special needs to send and receive objects during game play without the anxiety or pressure created by opponents or aggressive teammates. One parent who observed his son playing in a soccer crease referred to it as the "eye" in the middle of a hurricane. One of my colleagues called the crease area a competition "cocoon." It may also provide a safe practice area for individual or partner work while the main body of the class participates in a large group mass game.

Procedure: The teacher identifies students who may benefit from the crease area, and offers it as an option for a specific activity. The teacher then defines one crease area for each student who elects it by establishing clear boundaries. The most common use of crease areas is for team sports with opposing goals like soccer, hockey, lacrosse, and basketball. The most common area is a four-foot wide lane—one at each of the four corners of the playing area. In a gymnasium, this affords crease players to trap objects in their creases as they rebound from the walls. Teachers or trained peers can assist "trapping" and feeding the objects into the crease area. Crease players should have some limit to the time they work with the ball—either offensively or defensively. It helps to verbally call out, "shoot, pass, or dribble," to cue the students about their options. Especially during game play, crease players, by definition, get over-anxious and sometimes forget what their role is.

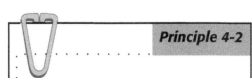

Principle 4-2

The option to shoot, pass, or dribble, is referred to as the trinity. These verbal cues prompt anxious students to help them make decisions under game-play pressure.

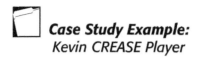

Case Study Example:
Kevin CREASE Player

Kevin uses an electric wheelchair and does not demonstrate good control using his newly fitted joystick controller. He chooses a crease area on the offensive side of the hockey field of play (indoor gymnasium). The crease is defined by a green line that runs parallel to the wall with four feet of space between the line and the wall. Kevin positions himself in the crease. Kevin has the ability to drive his chair into the ball, guiding it with a device resembling a crab claw mounted to his foot-rests. His teammates know that passing to Kevin guarantees a possession on the offensive side of the gym, so he receives several passes during the game. Once the ball enters the crease, defenders quickly run to block Kevin's shot. Once he gets the ball, he maneuvers it so that it rolls to a teammate. Kevin receives the ball as much as his peers in the main body of the action. He does not get any unfair advantage to score. The adaptation simply changes the environment so that he has an equal opportunity for participation. Kevin may practice to become a clock player with preparatory activities designed by the teacher.

CLOCK Concept

Definition: The clock is a verbal count by the teacher that provides a window of time in which all players except the clock player are restricted from moving their positions. In essence, all players except the clock player freeze their feet. This allows a student with special needs to manipulate a game object (ball or puck) and position him or herself for the trinity (pass, dribble, or shoot). Frozen players, especially defenders, need to be monitored to ensure they have not moved their position. Typically, defenders are allowed to move their torsos and arms to defend. In some rare cases with a student with significant limitations, the defenders

Instructional Tip 4-2

Note: Students in the main body of the class will accept these adaptations if they are presented positively by the teacher. If the teacher introduces adaptations in a condescending manner, students will get the message that they are not legitimate rules.

may need to freeze all movement. This is difficult to police, especially with competitive students.

Purpose: The clock changes the dynamic game play environment into a temporarily static environment. The duration of the clock is a function of the student's developmental ability. The student should be able to control and manipulate the object in less than ten seconds. This ensures a natural flow to the game play with minimal frustration by the main body of the class. Most students appreciate the opportunity to stop moving and rest for a few seconds during game play.

Procedure: The teacher determines which students have special needs making them eligible to be clock players. During practice time in the preparatory activities, the teacher establishes a baseline of time that each student may need to manipulate the object in the game. The teacher should set up small group activities so that the player can experience the pressure associated with defenders during competition. If the student can implement the trinity in less than ten seconds, he or she is a candidate to be a clock player.

Before game play begins, the teacher identifies the clock player (s) verbally to the class so they are prepared to freeze their positions. For students in secondary programs it is more appropriate to use the term "lock" instead of "freeze." Once the game object touches the student's body or equipment (chair, cane, walker) the whistle blows and possession is awarded the clock player. Once all players are locked, and the clock player signals readiness, the teacher counts aloud verbally (for a three-second player), "One thousand three, one thousand two, one thousand one, PLAY!" On the cue PLAY, all players resume regular play.

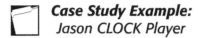

Case Study Example:
Jason CLOCK Player

Jason uses quad canes to walk and run. He has practiced in a small group and has agreed to be a five-second clock player during a game of five-on-five basketball. The other nine players, were selected by the teacher because they are mature players who like and accept Jason and his disability. During game play, Jason defends using his body, but must keep his canes below knee level. If the ball touches Jason's body or canes, the whistle blows and game play pauses. All players must lock their feet but are free to move their torsos and arms. The teacher trades the ball for Jason's right cane. The teacher counts down from five while Jason dribbles and moves toward the basket goal. He maneuvers carefully around bending and reaching opponents. On the count of "one" he takes a one-handed shot and misses. Game play resumes, and the teacher returns Jason's cane.

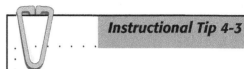

Instructional Tip 4-3

The teacher does not have to be the official in charge of the game and Jason's clock. If the students are grades K-3, older students should be trained as special peer teachers, and act in the role of the teacher in the above example. Students in secondary schools should be taught to officiate their own games, and a teammate should assist the clock player.

CHAPTER 5

Improvising Equipment

Adaptations have been presented to modify the task and the environment to meet the needs unique to individual students. While we think of modifying the environment and the task for student success as adapting, we think of using equipment creatively as improvising. Equipment will be described for our purposes as being traditional, alternative, or fabricated.

TRADITIONAL EQUIPMENT

Traditional equipment refers to equipment that is made available to physical education and recreational programs from retail stores and catalogs, and is designed for a specific sport or activity. The majority of the inventory for a program is likely to be the traditional variety. Basketballs, lacrosse sticks, and tennis racquets are examples of traditional sports equipment that many programs have in their inventories.

ALTERNATIVE EQUIPMENT

Alternative equipment is either traditional equipment used in a non-traditional way, or equipment that is not usually associated with athletic or recreational uses. The shuffleboard cue is a traditional piece of equipment for shuffleboard. During floor hockey, however, the shuffleboard cue may be used in an alternative way to guide a puck across the floor. Likewise, an electric leaf blower, which is not usually associated with volleyball, may be used to blow balloons or beach balls up into the air and over the net. It is a primary mission of this book to suggest practical uses for a variety of alternative equipment.

FABRICATED EQUIPMENT

Equipment may also be "fabricated," (home-made) from supplies purchased at a hardware or craft store. Only about one percent of the equipment in our inventory is fabricated, but it has been this one percent that seems to get the most attention. The primary reason I choose to fabricate equipment is that I recognize the need for a specific device that is not available through retail outlets and catalogs. That is, I see a need for a piece of equipment—and I create it! It is said that, "Necessity is the mother of invention." In our program, the "necessity" was to create parity for our students with disabilities. I have always accepted responsibility for equalizing the playing field for our students. There has been no greater reward for me in education than to see a student enjoy the thrill of equitable participation for the first time in his or her life. I have been fortunate to have facilitated this for hundreds of students over the years. I think my Uncle Nick would have been proud.

A second reason to fabricate equipment is that much of the traditional "retail" equipment is marked up many times over the cost to produce it. During our bowling unit, for example, I researched retail "bowling ramps" and found the least expensive ones to cost over $100.00. I fabricated each bowling ramp in our program for $2.50.

I have been successful at creating assistive devices for a variety of reasons. As I discuss in the foreword of this book, my uncles taught me the power of improvisation. Secondly, my high school physics teacher, Mr. Selway, helped provide me with the engineering skills necessary to turn ideas into working prototypes. Thirdly, the administration of the Kennedy Krieger Institute facilitated my creativity by granting me liability approval to put the equipment into use.

Universal Fabricated Equipment

The following describes the fabricated equipment that I used most frequently while working with students with disabilities. These devices are referred to as "universal" because they are appropriate to use for a variety of sports and activities. Part II, application, includes the uses specific to each sport.

Note: As with all fabricated equipment, the instructor should get clearance from the program administration to ensure compliance with liability regulations, before student use. Teachers should also use prudent judgment regarding safe practices and student supervision.

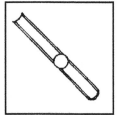

The Chute

Description: A longitudinal half-section of plastic PVC pipe, 8-10 feet in length.

Purpose: The general purpose is to provide a guided path along which a variety of objects can gain momentum with the assistance of gravity. Example: The chute may be used as a bowling ramp when rested on the knees of a student in a wheelchair.

Figure 5.1: Chute

Approximate Cost: $ 5.00 for two chutes.

Materials: One 8-10 foot length of 5-inch-diameter PVC pipe.

Procedure:

1. Cut the pipe longitudinally using a table saw to create two equal halves—or Chutes. The supplier may cut the plastic pipe for you.

3. Round the cut edges with a file for safety.

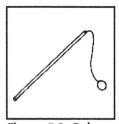

The Pole

Description: A 1" PVC pipe 8-10 feet in length.

Purpose: The pole serves two primary purposes. One is to extend the reach of a student. Example: Liz uses the Velcro on the tip of the pole to lift a tennis ball into the basketball goal. A second purpose is to provide a teacher-controlled striking device. A ball or object hangs from a string attached to the tip, resembling a fishing pole. The teacher can move the stick and control the flight of the ball toward the student to maximize striking success. Example: Kevin moves his left arm in a very uncontrolled, spastic manner. The teacher uses the pole to suspend a balloon just over the tennis net. The teacher uses the pole to guide the balloon such that Kevin may strike the balloon sending it over the net.

Figure 5.2: Pole

Approximate Cost: $ 2.00 per pole.
Materials: One 8-10 foot length of 1-inch-diameter PVC pipe.
Procedure:
1. Round the cut edges with a file for safety.
2. A variety of attachments may be used with the pole. In the examples provided, Velcro was placed on the tip of one pole, and a string was attached to the other.
3. The standard "fishing-pole" setup can be modified to become a "breakaway tether" by attaching the string to a clothes pin by the student's hand.
4. The student may then control the release of the ball by depressing the clothes pin.

The Arch

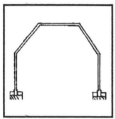

Figure 5.3: Arch

Description: A plastic arch 6 feet high and 4 feet wide. The legs of the arch sit in concrete bases (see procedure below).

Purpose: The general purpose is to provide a concrete representation of spatial boundaries. Students may work with the arches any time the concepts of "over," "under," or "through" are part of an activity or sport. Example: Maggie strikes the tennis ball with too much force, sending it out of bounds frequently. She has difficulty with the abstract concept of "swing easier." The teacher positions an arch in the middle of the court opposite Maggie. Maggie's task is to hit the ball softly enough that it bounces under the arch.

Approximate Cost: $ 10.00 per arch and base set.
Materials:
Two 4 foot lengths, and three 3 foot lengths of 1 inch PVC pipe.
Two 12 inch lengths of 1.5 inch PVC Pipe.
Four 45 degree angle joints.
1 can of PVC glue.
Two plastic buckets or containers at least 8 inches in diameter.
1 bag of concrete, water, and a shovel for mixing.
Procedure:
1. Glue the elbow joints and lengths of PVC pipe as shown in the diagram.
2. Allow several minutes for PVC glue to dry.
3. Mix concrete and fill each bucket 6-8 inches.
4. Tape one end of each length of 1.5 inch pipe. Insert the taped end into the concrete to the bottom of the container. The tape prevents concrete from entering the pipe. Allow the cement to harden for 24 hours. This pipe will act as a sleeve support into which one leg of the arch will rest. Each container forms one base. Each arch requires two bases.

The Pulley

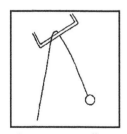

Figure 5.4: Pulley

Description: A loop of cord that glides over an overhead structure, such that a ball attached to one end of the cord may be moved by manipulating the other end of the cord.

Purpose: The general purpose is to provide a means for students with limited movement abilities to initiate and control the flight of a ball or object by manipulating a single cord. Example: Liz decides she wants to shoot a basketball into the regulation 10-foot goal. She does not have the balance or strength required to shoot the ball the required height. The teacher loops a tether cord over the orange rim and attaches a basketball to one end. Liz then pulls the cord back and fourth to make the ball swing. Liz coordinates her pulls such that the ball rises and falls through the basketball goal.

Approximate Cost: $ 20.00 per retail tether ball. $5.00 per roll of cord.

Materials:

1. One tether ball. (A ball with a "u" shaped bracket internally mounted)

2. A 20-foot length of cord.

Procedure:

Throw the tether cord across an overhead structure such that it will glide back and fourth in a pulley-like manner. The object is to move the ball up and down when the opposite end of the cord is pulled.

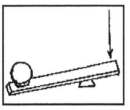

Figure 5.5: Catapult

The Catapult

Description: A wood lever that pivots on a fulcrum, much like a miniature playground "see-saw."

Purpose: The general purpose is to provide a device that will allow a student with limited movement abilities to forcefully propel a ball or object. Students with physical disabilities particularly enjoy getting major movement from minimal physical effort. This is the output-input principle.

Approximate Cost: $ 5.00 per catapult.

Materials:

1. One 12-24 inch length of 1X4 inch wood.

2. One triangular block of wood 2-4 inches high.

Procedure:

1. Rest the wood (lever) over the triangular block (fulcrum) such that one end of the wood is raised. Rest a lightweight ball (tennis balls work well) on the lowered side of the wood.

2. It may help to use a hole-saw to drill a shallow hole in the wood. This will help to keep the ball in place.

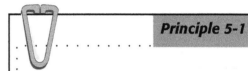

Principle 5-1

Input-Output Principle: Students with physical disabilities are motivated by getting maximum output (a ball flying across the gym) from minimal physical input (dropping a basketball onto the catapult lever).

3. Strike the raised end of the wood to propel the ball into the air.

4. Adjust the position of the triangle block to create different forces.

5. Students with limited movement abilities may drop a heavy ball onto the catapult. A basketball dropped from three feet has the ability to launch a tennis ball over 20 feet into the air.

Figure 5.6: Claw

The Claw

Description: A "U" shaped PVC device that mounts to the footrests of a wheelchair and glides a few inches from the floor. The "U" shape allows a student in a wheelchair to capture a rolling ball and control its movements.

Purpose: The general purpose is to provide students using wheelchairs the opportunity to control a rolling ball for games like soccer and floor hockey.

Approximate Cost: $ 25.00 per claw.

Materials:

1. One 12-inch length of 1X4 inch wood.

2. Two 12-inch lengths of 2-inch diameter PVC pipe.

3. Three 6-inch lengths of 2-inch diameter PVC pipe.

4. Four 45-degree angle joints.

5. PVC glue.

6. Two 2-inch "U" bolts with threads extending 4 inches.

7. Two 4 inch "C" clamps.

8. Two 4-inch steel angles. (Lengths will need to vary depending on height of wheelchair footrest from floor.)

9. Four sets of 1.5-inch machine screws/ nuts/washers.

Procedure:

1. Glue the PVC sections and 45-degree elbow joints as shown in the diagram.

2. Allow several minutes for the glue to dry.

3. Drill holes and fasten the PVC device to the wood using the "U" bolts as shown in the diagram.

4. Fasten the L-shaped steel brackets to the wood as shown in the diagram.

5. Clamp each L bracket to a wheelchair footrest. The claw should glide over the floor without dragging. It should be low enough to push a standard soccer ball.

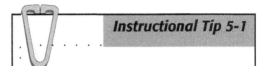

Instructional Tip 5-1

PVC (PolyVinylChloride) is one of the most valuable materials used to fabricate equipment, second only to Velcro and Duct Tape. PVC is the white plumbing pipe found in hardware stores and home improvement warehouses. It is inexpensive, lightweight, comes in various diameters and lengths, and is easy to cut. There are hundreds of attachments that may be purchased to glue on ends in a Lego-like fashion.

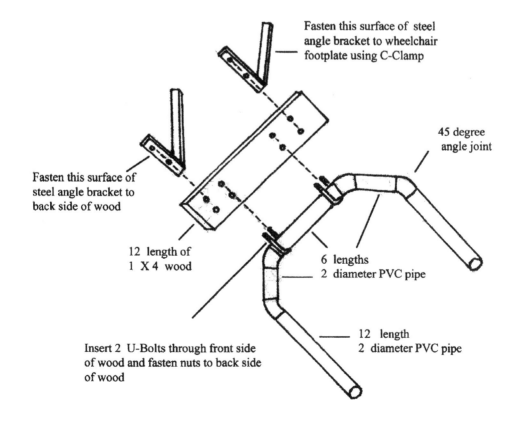

Fasten this surface of steel angle bracket to wheelchair footplate using C-Clamp

45 degree angle joint

Fasten this surface of steel angle bracket to back side of wood

12 length of 1 X 4 wood

6 lengths 2 diameter PVC pipe

12 length 2 diameter PVC pipe

Insert 2 U-Bolts through front side of wood and fasten nuts to back side of wood

Chart 5-1:
Universal Fabricated Equipment

DEVICE	Basketball	Volleyball	Soccer Hockey Lacrosse	Tennis Badminton	Baseball Softball
Chute	X	X	X	X	X
Tether-Pole	X	X	X	X	X
Arch	X	X	X	X	X
Pulley	X	X	X	X	X
Catapult	X	X		X	X
Claw			X		

PART II:
Application

Chapter 6: Basketball

Chapter 7: Volleyball

Chapter 8: Soccer

Chapter 9: Tennis

Chapter 10: Baseball

Basketball

Basketball is one of the most popular games in the country, and most physical education and recreation programs are equipped to offer basketball as an activity. Basketball is also one of the most adaptable games, requiring a minimal amount of equipment, and allowing for both individual and group play. The following chapter demonstrates the adaptation and improvisation that will help students with special needs overcome the challenges associated with playing basketball.

ADAPTING THE ENVIRONMENT AND TASK

Cognitive Adaptations

1. **The triangle.** Tape (inside court) or chalk (outside court) a triangle the size of the key area. This triangle space may be used to position students during lead-up games, or as the primary teaching tool for the progressive competitive levels. The triangle helps students understand positioning on an often confusing pattern of court lines.
2. **No-dribble rule.** Adopt this rule if students spend too much time dribbling. This rule helps students who are egocentric and need a reminder to share the ball with peers.
3. **Cones.** Use brightly colored cones to mark the corners of the court and the intersections of important lines. Cones may also be placed along a court line to reinforce the boundary concept. Cones placed along a boundary line form an imaginary "fence," which is exactly what it represents.
4. **Centerline rule.** During full-court games, do not permit the offensive team to move the ball across the half-court line until all defensive players are in position. Eliminating the fast-break will allow slow the pace of the game which is necessary for all but the most skilled athletes in class.
5. **"The 1ˢᵗ rule of basketball."** Explain that the most important rule in competitive basket-ball is, "Touch the ball, not the person!" Many of the intricate rules involving charging, holding, and fouling can be simplified for students with this simple statement.
6. **Visual and manipulative scoring.** Most people can not keep the running score for a game in their head. Provide a flip-chart scoring book for students to help them. A designated player for each team can quickly change the score between possessions. A more concrete strategy is to keep a container at each end of the court. Each time a team scores a goal, the ball is placed inside the container. Students may count the score as necessary for understanding.

7. *Jersey color coding.* Color coding teammates is critical to help students distinguish teammates from opponents. It is also helpful to color code the backboard as well.

Affective Adaptations

1. *Choice scoring.* Allow students to choose which scoring option is best for them. Backboard players earn one point when the ball they shoot contacts the backboard. They also get two points for contacting the rim, and three points for scoring a goal. Rim players may earn one point for their team if they contact the rim, and two points if they score a goal. Goal players score two points for a goal, and three points for a goal that is made from outside the three-point area. It is possible for students with different scoring privileges to play in the same game. You may be surprised to find just how many students will opt for the alternatives.

2. *Award of ball.* Many students do not handle the pressure of making foul shots well. Consider instead the policy of simply awarding the ball to the fouled player and then resuming play. Foul shooting also tends to slow down game play when working with unskilled players.

3. *Ability group teams.* Avoid traditional "team-captain" selection of teams. Inevitably the same students will consistently be picked last. Instead, adopt the routine of "ability grouping." This technique involves allowing students to pair themselves with a player of comparable ability. The partners then select opposite color jerseys and move to their respective areas. Teams will then be automatically "even" in terms of ability. In the case of an uneven number of students, the single player should partner with staff. This means that the staff person will need to be actively engaged in game-play. If there is only one teacher, the single student may consider rotating into game play with a group of three.

4. *Choice of competition or recreation (home games).* Students should be offered the opportunity to choose activities that are recreational or competitive. Basketball is a sport that affords students many recreational opportunities. Students may work individually, with a partner, or in a small group. Students that elect competitive game play should have supervision, structured progression, and some form of officiation.

5. *Choice passing.* Less skilled players are very anxious about passes that are thrown hard and direct. Students should be offered the option to choose how they receive passes from peers. Students who elect the "bounce pass" option play better without the fear of being hit by the ball, or missing a pass.

Sensorimotor Adaptations

1. *Beeper balls.* Beeper balls are usually made of foam and have an electronic beeping mechanism inserted into a cylinder shaped cavity. When the beeper is activated, it sounds a repetitive tone that visually impaired students use to track and locate balls. Beeper balls work well as hot balls during inclusive game play. Beepers may also be used outside of the ball. A beeper placed inside a crate or taped to a rim will signal visually impaired students on the location of the goal.

2. *Nerf balls.* Students who are visually impaired are vulnerable to being struck by equipment during class—particularly basketballs. Teacher judgment is critical to minimize the risk of regulation basketballs striking visually impaired students. Nerf balls should be used during inclusive activities to minimize the risk of injury.

3. *Flat rubber discs.* Flat rubber discs may be placed on the floor to create a type of "Braille" crease boundary. Hence, visually impaired students may choose the crease option for inclusive game play.

4. *Hand-arm signals.* Hearing impaired students benefit from a variety of hand-arm signals. It helps if players repeat signals from the official or teacher. If players get in the habit of raising their hands when the whistle sounds, the message gets to the student more effectively.

IMPROVISING EQUIPMENT

As discussed in Part I, psychomotor modifications occur through the process of improvising the equipment and facility. The following modifications are introduced relative to three categories of equipment—traditional, alternative, and fabricated.

Traditional Equipment

1. **Basketball sizes.** Basketballs are available in small, medium, and regulation sizes.
2. **Basketball texture.** Rubber basketballs provide durability and maintain a "grippy" texture longer than leather basketballs. Leather balls are preferred by students who want "regulation" game-play.
3. **Nerf balls.** While limited in their bounce qualities, Nerf balls are invaluable as safe alternatives when including students who are anxious and or vulnerable to injury by regulation basketballs.
4. **Geodesic mesh balls.** Geodesic balls are round and hollow, surrounded by molded cord in a mesh-like pattern. Students with spastic fingers can hold onto the mesh easily. Releasing is often successful by simply shaking or flinging the hand.
5. **Multicolored playground balls.** Students that have limited mobility spend the majority of their class time chasing basketballs that roll away from them. Playground balls may be partially deflated such that they keep their round "ball" quality, needed for shooting, but they flatten after hitting the floor, which limits the distance they roll away from the student.
6. **Standard basketball goals.** Basketball goals are sometimes adjustable. These may be set at varying heights to accommodate students of different abilities. There are also various adaptive goals that attach to existing non-adjustable systems, creating a lower goal.
7. **Wall bracket rim goals.** Wall brackets are aluminum sleeves that mount to the wall and accept generic basketball rims which slide into place. The brackets should be placed at varying heights on the wall to accommodate a variety of ability levels. They should also be aligned such that a set could support a full court game.
8. **Any-pole basketball goal.** Cost: Approximately $100.00. This is the commercial predecessor of the "U" bracket mount. It features an aluminum bracket that mounts to "any pole" less than six inches in diameter. The plastic knobs tighten the system from the back side of the backboard. Backboard and rim included. Safety note: This system is not intended for dunking activities. This product was initially fabricated by me, and later became popular enough for me to sell it to industry. I hope this inspires you to think outside of the box and start creating!

Alternative Equipment

1. **Trash cans (new & clean).** Trash cans and generic barrels may be used as low baskets in place of the traditional orange-hoop type of basketball goal. Students who use wheelchairs and require low basketball goals will frequently choose to shoot into barrels instead of rims.
2. **Mat craters** (Tumbling mats stood on edges and curved to form crater-like areas). These craters provide students a container for which to shoot soft basketballs. This is also enough space for in which one or more students may position themselves.
3. **Pulleys and tetherballs.** Ropes and cords can be rigged to act as pulleys such that a ball is attached to one end, and the student holds the other end. The object is for the student to move the ball using minimal physical manipulation. The tether can be attached to the wheelchair, as it might be for Kevin, or held in the hand, as Liz prefers. The most effective set-up is to simply throw a tether cord over a regulation basketball rim. The rim acts as the pulley—no wheel is necessary.

4. *Milk crates and fleece balls.* Just as the barrel and trash can provide alternative baskets, so too, does the milk crate. Fleece balls, which are actually puffy yarn balls the size of a softball, are easily manipulated by students, and several fit into one crate.
5. *Scooters.* Scooters equalize. That is, able-bodied students that sit on scooters are often disadvantaged by height and mobility such that students using wheelchairs, canes, and walkers can be competitive. It is interesting to observe an inclusive game where all able-bodied players struggle with the frustration of being scooter-disabled. It is equally interesting to observe the student using a wheelchair in a position of dominance and control.
6. *Wheelchairs.* Able-bodied students may elect to participate in an inclusive game of wheelchair basketball. As with scooters, the experience will facilitate an awareness of the challenges associated with a disabling condition.
7. *Cage balls.* Cageballs are oversized inflatable balls that are often multi-colored. Some come as large as 72-inches in diameter. Consider a cooperative basketball game in which the team needed to work together to balance the giant ball on a dixie cup. Cage balls may be used in a variety of individual activities involving pushing the ball into or onto objects like hoops, rings, or mats. This type of "giant basketball" is tailor made for Kevin, who can use his chair to safely push the ball.
8. *Beach balls.* Beach balls are lightweight, colorful, and have a special feature that few teachers utilize—the inflation stem. When pulled outward, the stem provides a handy appendage from which students can pick up, carry, and release. This is particularly helpful for students who are limited in their ability to reach from their wheelchair, cane, or walker.
9. *Parachute.* It is unfortunate that parachutes are frequently limited to early childhood and young children in most programs. The parachute is one of the most popular alternative pieces of sports equipment among middle and high school students in our programs.
10. *Shuffle cues & velcro.* Shuffle cues provide safe, lightweight poles for extending the reach of students. When velcro is attached to the tip, the extended pole takes on grasp and release properties. A student using a wheelchair may use the "pole," with velcro, to grab a lightweight ball from the floor, lift it toward the rim, and bang it such that the ball falls through the goal. Teachers may incorporate this skill into a variety of individual, preparatory, and inclusive activities.

Fabricated Equipment

1. *U-Bolt mount.* Cost about $ 2.50. per "U" Bolt. Purpose: To provide adjustable backboards from ground level to six-feet-high. Hardware stores carry a variety of "U" shaped bolts with threads on both the ends. Match the size of the "U" bolt to the factory drilled holes in a backboard. Slide the "U" bolt around a volleyball pole (or other stable pole), then slide the backboard onto the "U" bolt, allowing the two ends of the bolt to slide through the two factory holes in the backboard. Then attach two nuts and washers to the ends of the "U" bolt, securing the backboard in place. Safety Note 1: Pad the nuts and threads, as they may protrude outward on the playing side of the backboard causing an unsafe condition. Safety Note 2: This set up is intended for students to shoot balls into, and is not intended to support dunking activities.
2. *PVC chute.* See Part I for description. The chute provides a student-controlled path along which basketballs may reach a designated goal.
3. *Catapult.* See Part I for description. The catapult allows students to mechanically launch balls toward a designated goal.

IPI INCLUSION MODEL

Individual Activities

Basketball may be thought of as a thematic game involving putting an object in or through another object. Keeping this loose framework in mind, we develop activities that allow students to participate in activities that they can master individually, at their developmental levels. Students who master these activities may choose to participate in more advanced and "game-like" preparatory activities. Get out of your box and keep an open mind! Students love these activities.

1. ***Catapult basketball.*** Position the catapult such that a student can drop a basketball onto the raised arm of the lever. Position the fulcrum so the catapulted object (tennis balls work well) reaches the height of the basketball goal. The catapulted object may be launched toward targets on the wall, toward regulation basketball hoops, or into containers resting on the floor.

2. ***Chute basketball.*** (Resembles a bowling lane gutter.) The chute should be placed on a stack of mats such that it can pivot 360 degrees and tilt up and down. The student holds one end of the chute and places a ball at the end nearest him or her. The student may tilt or pivot the chute as the ball rolls toward the opposite end. The object is to use timing and positioning to make the ball drop into a designated spot or container. Tip: Use different types of balls to vary the speed with which it rolls along the chute. Tip: Mark the ends of the chute with colored tape for visual tracking.

3. ***Pulley basketball.*** Attach one end of the tether cord to a ball. The student holds onto the other end. Throw the tether cord over the basketball rim so it glides over the top in a pulley fashion. As the student pulls the tether cord, the ball will raise, lower, and swing. Games may be created that involve dropping the ball into a designated position or container. Advanced students may even pull the ball so that it drops into the basket. The tether cord may be attached to electric wheelchairs if the student is unable to manually hold or manipulate it.

4. ***Air hose basketball.*** Use the blower option on the vacuum to blow balloons or soap bubbles into the air and toward a target or container.

5. ***Pole basketball.*** Use the shuffle cue to lift balls toward the basketball goal. Velcro may be used to grasp and release balls. The ball will need to be banged or rubbed to remove it from the Velcro. A clothes pin may be attached to the pole near the student's hand, fixed such that it pinches a string to the pole. The string runs along the shaft, like on a fishing pole, and has a ball tied to its end. When the student presses the clothes pin, the string is released and the ball drops into a designated target or container.

6. ***Crate basketball.*** This activity involves placing or tossing balls into a crate positioned in a way that is challenging for the student. Crates are lightweight, and easily moved to a variety of places. They also hold many small balls, so a student may shoot several at a time.

Preparatory Activities

By definition, the nature of these activities prepares students for participation in the inclusive activity. Therefore, any activity that prepares a student for participation with the main body of the class may be considered preparatory. Students typically need practice selecting which primary competitive adaptation is best for them. They also need practice with small groups of peers at this level of participation.

1. ***Hot ball practice.*** The student gains familiarity with his or her selected ball by dribbling and or shooting independently.

2. ***Crease practice (trinity).*** The student works with a partner or small group to practice passing and receiving bounce passes within his or her identified crease space. Emphasis should be placed on performing under defensive pressure to ensure game-play readiness.

3. *Clock practice* (partner/small group). The student works with a partner or small group to practice dribbling, passing, receiving bounce passes, and shooting within the designated countdown duration. Staff need to help the student identify a challenging duration, in seconds. The duration should be less than 10 seconds before the student participates with the main body of the class.

4. *Hot goal with clock combo practice* (designated goal). Players choosing this option play as they would as a clock player, only they shoot at a basketball goal that is designated just for them.

Inclusive Activities

Recreational

1. *Parachute basketball.* Parachute basketball involves a group of 6-12 students who work together to fling the parachute upward such that the basketball in the center is catapulted toward a basketball goal. Points are awarded for contacting the support structure, the backboard, the rim, and for making a goal. This also provides teachable moments for principles of physics—momentum, angles, force, acceleration, rebound, and trajectory.

2. *Scooter basketball.* The student using a wheelchair, cane, or walker maintains the advantage of height and mobility in this game because able-bodied peers play while sitting on scooters. All rules for a small group game of basketball apply. The adaptation is the restricted mobility and height of the scooters for the able-bodied players.

3. *Wheelchair basketball.* Able-bodied players use wheelchairs to play against their peers who are skilled and practiced at using wheelchairs, canes, and walkers.

4. *HORSE.* This is a classic basketball game which is naturally inclusive. A small group of two-six players take turns making fancy shots. Once a shot is made, the student following must duplicate the technique to make the shot. If the shot is missed, a "letter" is earned—HORSE, respectively. Once as student earns all five letters, the game restarts. Note: It is neither appropriate nor necessary to "eliminate" students who earn HORSE. It is just as easy to restart the game, or transition to a new activity.

5. *Around the world.* This is another classic basketball game that is well suited for inclusive game-play. The floor (or court) is marked with four-eight spots layed out and numbered in chronological order. The spots may be labeled with names of people, places, or things. The original game labels the spots geographical locations—hence the name, Around The World. A student shoots from position 1. If the shot is made, the student moves to position 2. If the shot is missed, the student chooses to either give the ball to the next player, or risk taking a "chance" shot. Giving the ball to the next player allows the player to maintain the earned position. Making a chance shot allows the student to advance one space. Missing a chance shot moves the student back to start. The game restarts when a player makes it to all positions in the game.

Lead-up Activities

1. *Basketball tag* (dribbling, passing, catching). Each player dribbles a ball while moving around the gymnasium or court. A select few individuals are designated "taggers," who wear jerseys. Once a player is tagged, the basketball is placed between the feet, and he or she is considered "frozen." This cues classmates to make a bounce-pass to the "frozen" student to bring them back into the game. Frozen students must catch a bounce pass to re-enter the game. Students who helped unfreeze a peer may then pick up their peer's former ball and continue play. Students using wheelchairs, canes, and walkers may choose to be taggers or dribblers. They may also be immune to being tagged, but are tasked to unfreeze their able-bodied peers. Students with disabilities may also use hot balls to tag peers. By definition, the hot ball may not be touched by others, so making it an extension of the tagger's body is consistent with class rules. Tag is a universally adaptive and inclusive activity, and has been one of the most popular foundation-activities of our program.

2. *Capture basketball* (confronting opponent). The playing area is separated into three equally spaced zones. Students start in zone 1, where they select a basketball from a barrel. Zone 2 contains two-four players wearing jerseys who are designated defensive capturers. The capturers are instructed how to safely intercept the ball from the offensive players in zone 1. The object of the game is for players in zone 1 to dribble past the capturing players in zone 2 so that they can reach the safety of zone 3. Once in zone 3, students shoot until they make a basket. After a basket is made, the ball is place in a container, and students return to zone 1 to get a new ball and repeat the cycle. If a ball is captured, both the offensive player and the ball are returned to zone 1 where they may try again. Students using wheelchairs, canes, or walkers may participate in either offensive or capturing roles. Students using wheelchairs may wedge the ball between their feet instead of bounce-dribbling. In general, carrying may be substituted for dribbling in basketball.

3. *Crater basketball* (shooting). This activity involves small groups of students tasked with shooting large numbers of Nerf balls into their respective craters. Students using wheelchairs, canes, or walkers may position themselves inside the crater. Their objective is to collect and toss out the Nerf balls faster than their peers can shoot them in. Students with special needs may also elect to be the shooting players.

PRIMARY COMPETITIVE ADAPTATIONS

1. *Hot ball player.* Players choosing a hot ball may dribble and shoot within the competitive milieu of the class. This adaptation provides game-like stimulation for students with special needs who are not ready for fully inclusive play.

2. *Crease player.* Players choosing to be assigned a crease area pass and shoot in a static zone where other players are restricted. This affords a student with special needs the opportunity to incorporate closed skills into an open skill environment. Creases work best when they run parallel to the sideline, and are wide enough to provide a realistic chance of making a shot.

3. *Clock player.* Students choosing to be a clock player in basketball should be able to execute the trinity in ten seconds or less. More than ten seconds delays the game and increases player frustration. This option should be used when a player's skills will not permit him or her to pass or shoot without losing possession of the ball. This adaptation takes practice and patience by all players, and is best with the support of at least one engaged staff person.

4. *Hot goal clock combo.* This option is best when the player has all of the competitive skills necessary to play with the main body, except for the ability to shoot at the regulation ten-foot height. During the ten-second countdown, the student dribbles or moves to a designated goal. If the goal is scored, points are awarded the student's team. If the goal is missed, the opposing team gets possession.

PROGRESSIVE COMPETITIVE LEVELS SPORT SEQUENCE

Purpose: To provide structure to the positions and control to the pacing of the game.
 # Players: 3-5 per team, two teams
Equipment: One regulation basketball
Full court (may be modified for half court)
Taped or chalked triangles under each goal (as large as the key area)
Clearly marked half-court line
Colored jerseys for each team
At least one engaged staff member
Note: Students with special needs may participate using an inclusive activity at any progressive competitive level (PCL).

6-Level Basketball

Description: Students are arranged in groups of three to five players per team. Each playing area features a visible triangle in the area of the key directly under the basket. The lines of the triangle may be created using tape on gymnasium floors or chalk on asphalt courts. Games may be played half or full-court, as long as each goal includes a visible triangle. The equipment, including the height of the net and size of the ball, can be improvised or regulation, such that student success is maximized. The adaptations that follow involve modifications of the required skills (task), and both the court area and rules (environment). Students who are expected to participate in competitive Basketball activities should begin by playing Level-1 Basketball. Once the majority of the students in the group have demonstrated mastery at level-1, they should be allowed to transition to level 2-play.

Students may demonstrate mastery of level-1 or level-2 skills in a few minutes. The teacher should allow the students to progress when they demonstrate readiness, or the students will become frustrated and lose interest. In my experience, most intermediate classes progress through levels-1 and 2 in the introductory lesson. Most will progress through levels 3 and 4 during the second lesson. Ultimately, the majority of the students will reach their competitive limit at levels 4 or 5. By the conclusion of a Basketball unit, a select few students play at levels 1, 2, or 3. The majority of the students play at levels 4 or 5, while some advanced players compete at level 6. If the teacher develops the criteria for Progressive Levels appropriately, student performance should fit the standard bell curve parameters.

Level 1 Basketball:

1. All players on the defensive team must keep one foot inside the triangle under the goal in which they are defending.
2. All offensive players must receive a pass before the ball crosses the half-court line.
3. Offensive players may dribble, pass, or shoot while keeping the ball away from the defensive players who are restricted to the defensive triangle area.
4. Offensive players maintain possession until a goal is scored, the defense intercepts, or the ball travels out of bounds.
5. Once defensive players gain possession, offensive players travel to their respective triangle to play defense.
6. Play continues until time expires or an agreed-upon score is reached.

Level 2 Basketball:

1. One defensive player may travel outside of the defensive triangle each time the opposing team gains possession and begins their offensive movement toward the goal.
2. The defensive player may not cross the half-court line.
3. Offensive players are safe to pass and dribble until they cross the half-court line.
4. Staff should stop play for teachable moments that occur as a result of the interaction between the single defensive player and the offensive players.
5. Defensive players need to take turns outside of the triangle (numbering players works well).

Level 3 Basketball:

1. Two defensive players may travel outside of the defensive triangle to challenge the offense.
2. Defensive players may not cross the half-court line.
3. Offensive players need guidance to adjust to the increasing defensive presence.
4. Teachable moments should address personal fouls and appropriate offensive and defensive movements. This is the level of play where many students need to practice. Only after several cycles of possession are demonstrated without fouls and controversy, should the group move onto level 4.

Level 4 Basketball:

1. Three defensive players may travel outside of the defensive triangle to challenge the offense.
2. The offense must cross the half-court line within five seconds of the whistle.
3. Not all offensive players may receive a pass prior to shooting.
4. Once a change of possession occurs, the whistle sounds and play pauses while defensive players set up on their side of the court.
5. Play resumes on the whistle, once the defensive is set and ready for the offense.

Level 5 Basketball:

1. No defensive players are restricted to the defensive triangle.
2. Defensive players may not cross the half-court line until the offense moves the ball across first.
3. Regulation play occurs once the ball crosses the half-court line.
4. Once the ball is dead or possession changes, play pauses until the defense transitions to their respective side of the court.

Level 6 Basketball:

1. Regulation basketball game play.

Case Studies

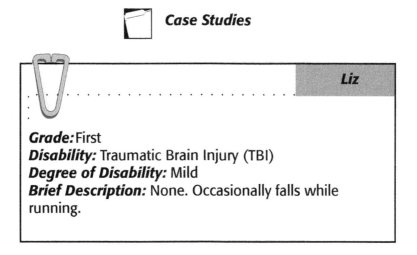

Liz

Grade: First
Disability: Traumatic Brain Injury (TBI)
Degree of Disability: Mild
Brief Description: None. Occasionally falls while running.

Basketball Participation:

Liz participates in the warm-up activities, but is anxious when working with the basketball. The teacher provides Liz with a hot ball to decrease her anxiety about classmates taking her ball away. The teacher provides a variety of group activities in which each student has a ball. During activities that require shooting, Liz chooses to work at the four-foot high wall mounted goal. By the end of the unit, Liz is successful playing recreational shooting games in a small group of peers. Her favorite basketball activity is basketball dribble-tag in which she gets to chase her classmates and capture their basketballs.

Kevin

Grade: Fourth
Disability: Orthopedic Impairment (OI), Cerebral Palsy
Degree of Disability: Severe and profound
Brief Description: Paralysis from the neck down. Learning to control spastic movement initiated from left shoulder to manipulate the joystick control on his electric wheelchair.

Basketball Participation:

Kevin begins his first lesson practicing tether-basketball with a 5th grade peer aide assigned by the teacher. The teacher transitions between the main body of the class and Kevin to provide feedback and praise. By the end of the class, Kevin is practicing a preparatory skill involving flicking a basketball from his wheelchair armrest into a plastic barrel. Kevin begins each new class with a different individual activity, and continues to practice his preparatory skills. During the 5th lesson, the teacher arranges a small group game in which Kevin plays using his skill in an inclusive manner. His teammates pass to Kevin by placing the ball on his armrest. Once the ball is placed, Kevin becomes a clock player, and moves adjacent to the barrel to score. With a count of five seconds, Kevin scores with 50 percent consistency, that is equal to his peers in the game. The other students on Kevin's team shoot at a regulation goal. They play with a Nerf basketball to decrease the risk of a rebound injuring Kevin, who is virtually defenseless. The group that works with Kevin receives positive praise and attention from the teacher. They are also given time to play with the main body of the class. By the end of the unit, Kevin participates in small group scooter basketball as well. He reports that it is fun to be taller than the rest of the players.

Maggie

Grade: Seventh
Disability: Orthopedic Impairment (OI), Cerebral Palsy
Degree of Disability: Moderate
Brief Description: Paraplegia affecting both legs, but not arms. Uses a wheelchair, walker, and/or quad canes, depending on the activity.

Basketball Participation:

Maggie chooses to skip the activities at the individual level and begin her work at the preparatory level. She excels at the warm-up games like dribble tag. Maggie is able to dribble and wheel at the same time. She plays well enough to be on a wheelchair league, but she is the only student in class using a wheelchair. Maggie tries all of the primary competitive adaptations during preparatory activities, and chooses to be a clock player for her first inclusive game. With each class Maggie is able to execute the trinity quicker, and by the end of the unit she only requires a count of two seconds. Maggie also chose to help those students electing non-competitive recreational shooting games to learn the rules to several games. Basketball is Maggie's favorite unit.

Phil

Grade: Eleventh
Disability: Orthopedic Impairment (OI), Below Knee Amputee
Degree of Disability: Moderate
Brief Description: Phil is learning to use his newly fitted prosthesis, and chooses to use his wheelchair depending on the activity. He is athletic and competitive.

Basketball

Participation:

Phil spends the first half of class participating with his prosthesis, and the second half using his wheelchair. This gives his leg a much-needed chance to rest and recover from the workout. During warm-ups, Phil takes his time and walks through the activities. Phil chooses to play competitively, and does not like to use the primary competitive adaptations. His peers do not offer him any special privileges or favors, but he accommodates with good positioning and making immediate passes or shots. When Phil transitions to his chair, he officiates competitive games. Phil also spends a part of each class working at the preparatory level, practicing his shooting from various distances from the goal. Phil's limited mobility has forced him to develop into one of the most accurate shooters in the program.

Chart 6-1:
Basketball Activities by Degree of Disability

	Mild	Moderate	Severe
Individual			
Catapult Basketball		X	X
Chute Basketball		X	X
Pulley Basketball		X	X
Air Hose Basketball		X	X
Pole Basketball		X	X
Crate Basketball		X	X
Preparatory			
Hot Ball Practice	X	X	X
Crease Practice	X	X	X
Clock Practice	X	X	
Hot-Clock Combo	X	X	
Inclusive			
Scooter Basketball	X	X	X
Parachute Basketball	X	X	X
Wheelchair Basketball	X	X	X
HORSE	X	X	X
Around the World	X	X	X
Basketball Tag	X	X	X
Capture Basketball	X	X	X
Crater Basketball	X	X	X
PCL Levels 1-5	X	X	

CHAPTER 7

Volleyball

Volleyball is played competitively, recreationally, and leisurely in a variety of environments, including gymnasiums, beaches, and neighborhood backyards. It may be played by partners, small groups, or teams with 10 - 15 players each. Volleyball requires minimal equipment, and the basic rules are easy to understand. Most physical education and recreation instructors agree volleyball is a versatile game that could easily be enjoyed by children and adults of all ages and abilities—so why isn't it?

The truth is, many educators fail to present volleyball to students in developmentally appropriate stages. The result is that students are expected to play the game at its most competitive level, whereby the majority are less than successful. A select few students will play using appropriate techniques, but most will punch, swing, slap, and carry the ball in an attempt to get it over the net—and save face from the embarrassment and ridicule of a missed hit. Regulation equipment and regulation rules will leave most students with red forearms, jammed fingers, and bruised egos. For many students with special needs, regulation volleyball play is not appropriate. The following chapter demonstrates the adaptation and improvisation that will help students with special needs overcome the challenges associated with volleyball.

ADAPTING THE ENVIRONMENT AND TASK

Cognitive Adaptations

1. **Position numbers.** Tape (inside court) or chalk (outside court) position numbers on the court such that students have a visual reference for rotating.
2. **Boundary highlights.** Use cones to help students distinguish the volleyball lines from the various other lines on the floor.
3. **Electric fence.** Students will associate electricity with, "Do not touch," which helps them remember net rules.
4. **Three-people touch rule.** Explain that no more than three students may touch the ball before it is returned over the net. This clarifies the rule for students who catch and pass the ball.
5. **Earning the serve rule.** Students will become frustrated that they are not earning points when the opposing team makes an error while serving. It is the teacher's responsibility to help students understand that they did earn something. If a team errors while serving, explain to the other team, "You earned the serve!" Follow with two verbal cues, "Rotate," and "Serving team may earn points."

6. **Calling the score.** Most people can not keep the running score for a game in their head. Volleyball, like other net activities, provides for frequent verbal reminders of the score. Each server should be required to verbally call the score before each serve. Failure to call the score should result in a loss of serve.
7. **Modified trinity.** Provide the verbal cues, "Pass," or "Over," to students who catch the ball. The excitement of the game will leave some students unable to make quick decisions, which will frustrate teammates.

Affective Adaptations

1. **Choice serving.** Students with emotional challenges do not tolerate serving failure well. Offer students the opportunity to choose the distance from the net for their serve. Encourage underhand-open-palm serving for greater control.
2. **Position grids.** The single greatest cause for fights and arguments in volleyball is students violating other students personal space. Typically, an aggressive player will run into other players' areas to make the play. Taped or chalked lines provides a visual reference to assist students with "playing their own positions."
3. **Ability group teams.** Avoid traditional "team-captain" selection of teams. Inevitably the same students will consistently be picked last. Instead, adopt the routine of "ability grouping." This technique involves allowing students to pair themselves with a player of comparable ability. The partners then select opposite color jerseys and move to their respective areas. Teams will then be automatically "even" in terms of ability. In the case of an uneven number of students, the single player should partner with staff. This means that the staff person will need to be actively engaged in game play. If there is only one teacher, the single student may consider rotating into game play with a group of three.
4. **Receiver choice.** Some students will not be comfortable receiving an airborne ball. Allow these students the opportunity to designate a "buddy" who can catch balls dropping into their zone. "Buddies" should pass the ball to the player who they assisted.

Sensorimotor Adaptations

1. **Beeper balls.** Beeper balls are usually made of foam and have an electronic beeping mechanism inserted into a cylinder shaped cavity. When the beeper is activated, it sounds a repetitive tone that visually impaired students use to track and locate balls. Beeper balls work well as hot balls during inclusive game play.
2. **Nerf balls.** Students who are visually impaired are vulnerable to being struck by equipment during class—particularly volleyballs. Teacher judgment is critical to minimize the risk of regulation volleyballs striking visually impaired students. Nerf balls should be used during inclusive activities to minimize the risk of injury.
3. **Flat rubber discs.** Flat rubber discs may be placed on the floor to create a type of "Braille" crease boundary. Hence, visually impaired students may choose the crease option for inclusive game play. These discs are also useful for creating position grids.
4. **The grab-and-toss.** Visually impaired students are allowed to grab the net, to gain spatial perspective, before they hit or toss the ball over the net.
5. **Safety buddy.** A buddy may be assigned to protect visually impaired students from being struck by airborne balls.
6. **Scoring.** Score should be shown visually and called verbally to assist students with hearing and vision impairments.

IMPROVISING EQUIPMENT

As discussed in Part I, psychomotor modifications occur through the process of improvising the equipment and facility. The following modifications are introduced relative to three categories of equipment—traditional, alternative, and fabricated.

Traditional Equipment

1. **Volleyball sizes.** Volleyballs are available in "over-sized" and "under-weight" varieties. The best "trainer" balls are twice the size of the regulation volleyball. Many simply have a leather cover over a latex balloon bladder.
2. **Volleyball texture.** Rubber volleyballs provide durability, water-resistance, and maintain a "grippy" texture longer than leather volleyballs. However, rubber and vinyl volleyballs are less forgiving on students' forearms and wrists than leather. Leather balls are preferred by students who want "regulation" game play.
3. **Nerf balls.** While limited in their bounce qualities, Nerf balls are invaluable as safe alternatives when including students who are anxious and or vulnerable to injury by regulation volleyballs.
4. **Geodesic mesh balls.** Geodesic balls are round and hollow, surrounded by molded cord in a mesh-like pattern. Students with spastic fingers can hold onto the mesh easily. Releasing is often successful by simply shaking or flinging the hand.
5. **Multicolored playground balls.** Students who have limited mobility spend the majority of their class time chasing volleyballs that roll away from them. Playground balls may be partially deflated such that they keep their round "ball" quality, needed for game play, but they flatten after hitting the floor, which limits the distance they roll away from the student.
6. **Standard volleyball nets** are usually height adjustable. These may be set at varying heights to accommodate students of different abilities. It is often desirable to allow the net to sag in the center, providing a less challenging area for students with limited tossing or hitting abilities.
7. **Global ball nets.** Global ball nets feature three large holes, each the diameter of the net width, equally spaced along the length of the net. The holes provide an area in which students sitting in wheelchairs may send balls through to the opponent, while the net height remains regulation for non-disabled players.

Alternative Equipment

1. **Mat craters** (Tumbling mats stood on edges and curved to form crater-like areas). These craters provide students a container for which to volley or serve soft volleyballs. One or more students may position themselves inside the mat crater to repel or toss out volleyballs as they enter. This is a particularly stimulating space for students in wheelchairs, as they are likely to be bombarded with incoming volleyballs.
2. **Scooters.** Scooters equalize. That is, able-bodied students who sit on scooters are often disadvantaged by height and mobility such that students using wheelchairs, canes, and walkers can be competitive. It is interesting to observe an inclusive game where all able-bodied players struggle with the frustration of being scooter-disabled. It is equally interesting to observe the student using a wheelchair in a position of dominance and control. The net may be lowered to the height of a tennis net to assist students using scooters.
3. **Electric leaf blower or vacuum** (reversed airflow). Use the blower to send balloons, beach balls, or soap bubbles over the net.
4. **Wheelchairs.** Able-bodied students may elect to participate in an inclusive game of wheelchair volleyball. As with scooters, the experience will facilitate an awareness of the challenges associated with a disabling condition.
5. **Cage balls.** Cage balls are oversized inflatable balls that are often multi-colored. Some come as large as 72 inches in diameter. Consider a cooperative volleyball game in which the team needed to work together to balance the giant ball on a dixie cup. Cage balls may be used in a variety of individual activities involving pushing the ball into or onto objects like hoops, rings, or mats. This type of "giant volleyball" is tailormade for Kevin, who can use his chair to safely push the ball.

6. **Beach balls.** Beach balls are lightweight, colorful, and have a special feature that few teachers utilize—the inflation stem. When pulled outward, the stem provides a handy appendage from which students can pick up, carry, and release. This is particularly helpful for students who are limited in their ability to reach from their wheelchair, cane, or walker. The stem is also helpful for underhand serving. Students hold the ball by the stem with one hand, and strike with the other.

7. **Parachute.** It is unfortunate that parachutes are frequently limited to early childhood and young children in most programs. The parachute is one of the most popular alternative pieces of sports equipment among middle and high school students in our programs. The parachute may be used by groups of students to launch a volleyball up and over the volleyball net.

8. **Shuffle cues and Velcro.** Shuffle cues provide safe, lightweight, poles for extending the reach of students. When Velcro is attached to the tip, the extended pole takes on gasp and release properties. A student using a wheelchair may use the "pole," with Velcro, to grab a lightweight ball from the floor, lift it over the net, and bang it such that the ball falls into the opponents court. Teachers may incorporate this skill into a variety of individual, preparatory, and inclusive activities.

Fabricated Equipment

1. **PVC Chute.** See Part I for description. The chute provides a student-controlled path along which balls may reach a designated goal. The chute may be used with a low net to send balls to a partner or opponent.

2. **Catapult.** See Part I for description. The catapult allows students to mechanically launch balls over the net with minimal physical effort.

3. **The arch.** The arch may be used as a concrete spatial reference which communicates boundaries for striking. Students may hit the ball under the arch or over the arch. Tetherballs may also be suspended from the arch to provide catching, tossing, and striking practice.

4. **The pole.** The teacher holds the pole, much like a fishing pole, with a lightweight ball attached to the pole by a length of cord. The teacher uses the pole to "hover" the ball in front of the student, making it easier to hit. The teacher may also use the pole to move the ball over the net following a hit by the student. This is particularly helpful when the student does not hit the ball with enough force to send it over the net.

IPI INCLUSION MODEL

Individual Activities

Volleyball may be thought of as a thematic game involving putting an object over another object. Keeping this loose framework in mind, we develop activities that allow students to participate in activities that they can master individually, at their developmental levels. Students who master these activities may choose to participate in more advanced and "game-like" preparatory activities. Get out of your box and keep an open mind! Students love these activities.

1. **Catapult volleyball.** Position the catapult such that a student can drop a volleyball onto the raised arm of the lever. Position the fulcrum so the catapulted object (tennis balls work well) is launched over the volleyball net. The catapulted object may be launched toward targets on the wall, over regulation nets, or into containers resting on the floor.

2. **Chute volleyball.** (Resembles a bowling lane gutter.) The chute should be placed on a stack of mats such that it can pivot 360 degrees and tilt up and down. The chute may be positioned over a low net. The student holds one end of the chute and places a ball at the end nearest him or her. The student may tilt or pivot the chute as the ball rolls toward the opposite end. One objective may be to simply control the chute such that the ball drops

over the net. Another objective may be to maneuver the chute so the ball drops into a designated area. A third objective may be to send the ball to a partner, who would return it along the chute. Tip: Use different types of balls to vary the speed with which it rolls along the chute. Tip: Mark the ends of the chute with colored tape for visual tracking.

3. *Pulley volleyball.* Attach one end of the tether cord to a ball. The student holds onto the other end. Throw the tether cord over a basketball rim (or some other object positioned over a volleyball net) so it glides over the top in a pulley fashion. As the student pulls the tether cord, the ball will raise, lower, and swing. Games may be created that involve dropping the ball into a designated position or container. Advanced students may even pull the ball so that it moves up and over the volleyball net. The tether cord may be attached to electric wheelchairs if the student is unable to manually hold or manipulate it.

4. *Air hose volleyball.* Use an electric leaf blower, or the blower option on a vacuum, to blow balloons or soap bubbles into the air and over the net.

5. *Pole volleyball.* Use the shuffle cue to lift balls toward the volleyball net. Velcro may be used to grasp and release balls. The ball will need to be banged or rubbed to remove it from the Velcro. A clothes pin may be attached to the pole near the student's hand, fixed such that it pinches a string to the pole. The string runs along the shaft, like on a fishing pole, and has a ball tied to its end. When the student presses the clothes pin, the string is released and the ball drops.

6. *Crater volleyball.* This activity involves using a mat crater as a collection space for Nerf volleyballs that are hit or served into the crater. Students using assistive devices enjoy being selected as the students who are positioned inside the crater to receive and return the balls. Note that the incoming balls will likely strike the students inside the craters, which adds to the excitement of the activity. Use Nerf-type or soft balls for safety.

Preparatory Activities

By definition, the nature of these activities prepares students for participation in the inclusive activity. Therefore, any activity that prepares a student for participation with the main body of the class may be considered preparatory. Students typically need practice selecting which primary competitive adaptation is best for them. They also need practice with small groups of peers at this level of participation.

1. *Hot ball practice.* The student gains familiarity with his or her selected ball by catching, tossing, and striking it individually.

2. *Crease practice* (trinity). The student works with a partner or small group to practice passing and receiving bounce passes within his or her identified crease space. Emphasis should be placed on catching without dropping the ball, passing to a partner and sending the ball over the net.

3. *Clock practice* (partner/small group). The student works with a partner or small group to practice catching, passing, receiving bounce passes, and sending the ball over the net—all within the designated countdown duration. Staff need to help the student identify a challenging duration, in seconds. The duration should be less than 10 seconds before the student participates with the main body of the class.

Note: Students with special needs should play at a low net with a small group of peers before entering an inclusive game. This will help them to understand the rules, as well as provide opportunities to practice their modified skills under "dynamic" game-play pressure.

Inclusive Activities

Recreational

1. **Global volleyball.** This activity features a volleyball net with three giant holes sewn into netting. Each team remains on its side of the net, along with three opponents who are positioned as goal-tenders in front of the holes (craters). Each team attempts to throw the ball through the holes (craters), which may be blocked by the goal tenders. The holes provide a natural adaptation for students with special needs. The holes are easy to reach as offensive shooters, and easy to block as defenders. Students using wheelchairs are especially effective as blockers. Students using canes and walkers, too, can play competitively with one hand support hand and one game-play hand.

2. **Parachute volleyball.** Parachute volleyball involves a group of 6-12 students who work together to fling the parachute upward such that the volleyball in the center is catapulted over the net. Points may be awarded for contacting the net and sending the ball over the net. This also provides teachable moments for principles of physics—momentum, angles, force, acceleration, rebound, and trajectory.

3. **Scooter volleyball.** The student using a wheelchair, cane, or walker maintains the advantage of height and mobility in this game because able-bodied peers play while sitting on scooters. All rules for a small group-game of volleyball apply. The adaptation is the restricted mobility and height of the scooters for the able-bodied players.

4. **Wheelchair volleyball.** Able-bodied players use wheelchairs to play against their peers who are skilled and practiced at using wheelchairs, canes, and walkers.

Lead-up Activities

1. **Volleyball tag** (Sending balls over the net). Each player carries a ball while moving around the gymnasium or court on a designated side of the net. A select few individuals are designated "taggers," who wear jerseys. Once a player is tagged, he or she needs to hit or toss the ball over the net. Players without volleyball must remain "frozen" until a teammate carries an extra ball over to the frozen player. The teacher should verbally cue classmates to hand deliver a ball or bounce pass a ball to "frozen" students so they may re-enter the game. Students using wheelchairs, canes, or walkers may choose to be taggers or runners. They may also be immune to being tagged, but are tasked to unfreeze their able-bodied peers. Students with disabilities may also use hot balls to tag peers. By definition, the hot ball may not be touched by others, so making it an extension of the tagger's body is consistent with class rules. Tag is a universally adaptive and inclusive activity, and has been one of the most popular foundation-activities of our program.

2. **Trashball** (Clean out the backyard). This game is simple, yet students of all ages and abilities enjoy it. Position one team on each side of a net, and flood the gymnasium floor with soft volleyballs. Students are directed to hit or toss volleyballs into their opponents' court. Add music, and stop all play when the music stops. A quick survey of the floor will tell which team is hitting more balls than the other. Re-start the music and cue students as required.

3. **Crater serving.** This activity involves small groups of students tasked with serving large numbers of Nerf balls into their respective craters. Students using wheelchairs, canes, or walkers may position themselves inside the crater. Their objective is to collect and toss out the Nerf balls faster than their peers can serve them in. Students with special needs may also elect to be the shooting players.

4. **Volleyball dodge.** Position a net high over students heads (balls will be sent under) or low to the floor (balls will be sent over). This dodge game should be played with nerf-like volleyballs. Students are positioned on each side of the net, forming two teams. The object is to strike the ball over or under the net so that it hits an opponent. Students are encouraged to use volleyball strikes including the serve, set, or bump to send the ball toward

opponents. Students who are hit need to join their opponents' team. Continue until all players are on one side of the net, or for a designated duration.

PRIMARY COMPETITIVE ADAPTATIONS

1. *Hot ball player.* Players choosing a hot ball may receive, pass, and send balls over the net within the competitive milieu of the class. This adaptation provides game-like stimulation for students with special needs who are not ready for fully inclusive play.
2. *Crease player.* Players choosing to be assigned a crease area pass and receive volleyballs in a static zone where other players are restricted. This affords a student with special needs the opportunity to incorporate closed skills into an open skill environment. Volleyball creases work best when they are positioned center court, where the net sags at its lowest point, providing a realistic chance of sending the ball over the net. Creases may also be positioned in front of a specific hole (crater) in a global ball net.
3. *Clock player.* Students choosing to be a clock player in volleyball should be able to execute the trinity in ten seconds or less. More than ten seconds delays the game and increases player frustration. This option should be used when a player's skills require that he or she catch the ball before passing, throwing, or striking it over the net. This adaptation takes practice and patience by all players, and is best with the support of at least one engaged staff person.

PROGRESSIVE COMPETITIVE LEVELS SPORT SEQUENCE

Purpose: To provide structure to the positions and control to the pacing of the game.
 # Players: 4-12 players per team, two teams
Equipment: One regulation or adapted volleyball
             Volleyball net positioned regulation height or lower
             Court boundaries highlighted with cones or flat discs
             Clearly marked center line
             Position numbers taped or chalked on court
             Position grids taped or chalked on court
             Colored jerseys for each team
             At least one engaged staff member

Note: Students with special needs may participate using an inclusive activity at any progressive competitive level (PCL).

7-Level Volleyball

Description: Students are arranged in standard volleyball formation, on either a standard or modified court. The equipment, including the net and ball, can be improvised or regulation, such that student success is maximized. The adaptations that follow involve modifications of the required skills (task), and both the court area and rules (environment). Students who are expected to participate in competitive volleyball activities should begin by playing level 1 volleyball. Once the majority of the students in the group have demonstrated mastery at level 1, they should be allowed to transition to level 2 play.

Students who have not mastered the skills for a particular level should be allowed to continue playing at their respective level while the remainder of the group moves to the next difficulty level. It is common to have students playing at different levels in the same game. For example, in any given game, Terrell is allowed to catch the ball on one bounce, while Maggie may only catch the ball in the air. The remainder of the players may not be allowed to catch the ball at all.

Students may demonstrate mastery of level 1 or level 2 skills in a few minutes. The teacher should allow the students to progress when they demonstrate readiness, or the students will become frustrated and lose interest. In my experience, most intermediate classes progress through levels 1 and 2 in the introductory lesson. Most will progress through levels 3 and 4 during the second lesson. Ultimately, the majority of the students will reach their competitive limit at levels 4 or 5. By the conclusion of a volleyball unit, a select few students play at levels 1, 2, or 3. The majority of the students play at levels 4 or 5, while some advanced players compete at levels 6 or 7. If the teacher develops the criteria for progressive levels appropriately, student performance should fit the standard bell curve parameters.

Level 1: Bounce-Catch Volleyball
1. The ball is put into play with a toss or throw from the right side of the court.
2. The server may position him or herself any distance from the net to get the ball over.
3. The receiving team may catch the ball on one bounce, or in the air. Only three players are allowed to touch the ball before the ball is returned over the net.
4. The ball may bounce once when it is passed between players on the same team.
5. The ball may be returned over the net with a toss or a strike.
6. Following a side-out, the team earning the serve rotates players as usual.
7. Game play continues until:
   A) time expires
   B) a predetermined score is reached
   C) the majority of the students demonstrate readiness to move to the next difficulty level.

Level 2: Catch Volleyball
1. All rules for level 1 apply, except:
2. Players may not let the ball bounce during the course of game play.
3. Players may catch the ball or strike the ball during game play.

Level 3: Serve Volleyball
1. All rules for level 2 apply except:
2. The volleyball must be put into play using the underhand serve technique.
3. The server may choose to serve from one of three positions—at the net, at mid-court, or at the baseline (regulation).

Level 4: Set Volleyball
1. All rules for level 3 apply except:
2. The ball may not be tossed over the net.
3. Players may catch a ball that is returned over the net, however the player that chooses to send it over the net must demonstrate a regulation "set" or strike.
4. The player that chooses to strike the ball may toss the ball to him or herself to execute the "set" or strike.

Level 5: Bump Volleyball
1. All rules for level 4 apply except:
2. The receiving team may not catch the ball as it is served or returned over the net.
3. The first and last touch when playing a ball must be a "set," "bump," or regulation strike.
4. A player on the receiving team may "bump" or "set" the ball to a teammate whom may catch the ball. This provides a safety net for the players with limited striking control.
5. The ball must be "set" or "bumped" over the net to resume game play.

Level 6: Bump-Set Volleyball
1. All rules for level 5 apply except:

2. The ball may not be caught at any time during game play.
3. Players may return the ball over the net with any strike technique.

Level 7: Regulation (Bump-Set-Spike) Volleyball
1. Regulation game play.
2. Players are encouraged to demonstrate the bump-set-spike combination during game play.

Case Studies

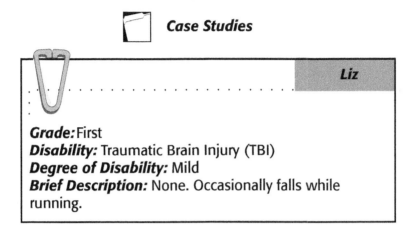

Grade: First
Disability: Traumatic Brain Injury (TBI)
Degree of Disability: Mild
Brief Description: None. Occasionally falls while running.

Volleyball Participation:

Liz loves volleyball activities. She spends the first few lessons working with her peers who use wheelchairs. She helps the students who require individual activities, like the chute and the catapult. Her favorite individual activity includes hitting the volleyball suspended by the tether pole. The teacher encourages Liz to work on her underhand serving with a partner. She is most successful pinching the stem of the beach ball with her left hand while she strikes with her right. During preparatory activities, Liz excels at catching passes from her peers. She is also able to throw the ball over the volleyball net at its regulation height! Liz participates in both volleyball dodge and volleyball tag without adaptations. She also has a good time being bombarded with Nerf volleyballs inside the mat crater. By the end of the unit, Liz is able to consistently underhand serve Nerf balls over the regulation volleyball net during the trashball activity.

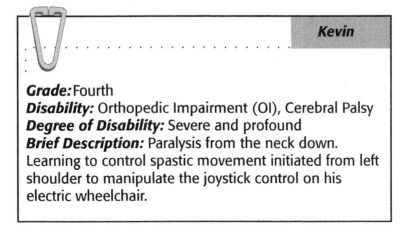

Grade: Fourth
Disability: Orthopedic Impairment (OI), Cerebral Palsy
Degree of Disability: Severe and profound
Brief Description: Paralysis from the neck down. Learning to control spastic movement initiated from left shoulder to manipulate the joystick control on his electric wheelchair.

Volleyball Participation:

Kevin begins his first lesson practicing catapult volleyball with a 5th grade peer aide assigned by the teacher. In this activity, Kevin uses his arm to knock a rubber bowling ball onto the raised arm of the lever, sending a leather volleyball up and over the net. The teacher transitions between the main body of the class and Kevin to provide feedback and praise. By the end of the class, Kevin is practicing a preparatory skill involving striking a balloon suspended by a tether pole. Kevin's aide maneuvers the pole to maximize his chances of hitting the balloon with his spastic arm movements. When he hits the balloon, the aide lifts the balloon up and over the net. This is the preparatory skill that the teacher will use to include Kevin in inclusive gameplay. Kevin begins each new class with a different individual activity, and continues to practice his preparatory skills. During the 5th lesson, the teacher arranges a small group game in which Kevin plays using the tether pole in an inclusive manner. His teammates pass to Kevin by placing the leather volleyball in his lap. Once the ball is placed, Kevin becomes a clock player, and moved his chair up to the net. With a count of ten seconds, Kevin was able to contact the suspended balloon three out of five times. After 10 seconds, or a hit, a teammate removes the game ball from Kevin's lap to resume game play. The teacher is positioned next to Kevin to intercept balls that may hit Kevin, who is virtually defenseless. The group that works with Kevin receives positive praise and attention from the teacher. They are also given time to play with the main body of the class. By the end of the unit, Kevin participates in small group global ball as well. He reports that he likes to use his chair to block the holes (craters).

Maggie

Grade: Seventh
Disability: Orthopedic Impairment (OI), Cerebral Palsy
Degree of Disability: Moderate
Brief Description: Paraplegia affecting both legs, but not arms. Uses a wheelchair, walker, and/or quad canes, depending on the activity.

Volleyball Participation:

Maggie chooses to skip the activities at the individual level and begin her work at the preparatory level. She excels at the warm-up games like volleyball tag. Maggie is able to hold the ball and wheel at the same time. She plays well enough to be on a wheelchair league, only she is the only student in class using a wheelchair. Maggie tries all of the primary competitive adaptations during preparatory activities, and chooses to be a crease player for her first inclusive game. With each class Maggie is able to send the ball over the net with greater efficiency. By the end of the unit she is able to leave her crease and strike the ball over the net at regulation height. Although she enjoys volleyball, she reports that serving and tossing makes her arms tired. She spends a part of each class helping her more restricted peers who elect individual activities. Her favorite activity is working with her classmates as they use the leaf blower to send balloons flying over the net.

Phil

Grade: Eleventh
Disability: Orthopedic Impairment (OI), Below Knee Amputee
Degree of Disability: Moderate
Brief Description: Phil is learning to use his newly fitted prosthesis, and chooses to use his wheelchair depending on the activity. He is athletic and competitive.

Volleyball Participation:

Phil spends the first half of class participating with his prosthesis, and the second half using his wheelchair. This gives his leg a much-needed chance to rest and recover from the workout. During warm-ups, Phil takes his time and walks through the activities. Phil chooses to play competitively, and does not like to use the primary competitive adaptations. His peers do not offer him any special privileges or favors, but he accommodates with good positioning and making immediate passes or hits. When Phil transitions to his chair, he officiates competitive games. Phil also spends a part of each class working at the preparatory level, practicing his sets and bumps. Phil's limited mobility has forced him to develop into one of the most accurate hitters in the program. Even so, he still participates at level 5 volleyball—the highest level in the class. Most of his peers play at volleyball levels 3 and 4.

Chart 7-1:
Volleyball Activities by Degree of Disability

	Mild	Moderate	Severe
Individual			
Catapult Volleyball		X	X
Chute Volleyball		X	X
Pulley Volleyball		X	X
Air Hose Volleyball		X	X
Pole Volleyball		X	X
Crater Volleyball		X	X
Preparatory			
Hot Ball Practice	X	X	X
Crease Practice	X	X	X
Clock Practice	X	X	
Inclusive			
Global Volleyball	X	X	X
Parachute Volleyball	X	X	X
Scooter Volleyball	X	X	X
Wheelchair Volleyball	X	X	X
Volleyball Tag	X	X	X
Trashball Volleyball	X	X	X
Crater Serve Volleyball	X	X	X
Volleyball Dodge	X	X	X
PCL Levels 1-7	X	X	X

CHAPTER 8

Soccer

Soccer, like basketball, is an "invasive" sport involving two teams working competitively against each other to score goals. Soccer, however, is played, for the most part, without using the hands. This makes game play challenging for those students who use assistive devices, and or have orthopedic impairments involving the legs and feet. Wheelchair basketball is popular in adaptive athletic programs, but wheelchair soccer is seldom considered a viable option. The obvious reason is the impracticality of pushing a regulation soccer ball with a wheelchair. Students who use canes or walkers are even less likely to have opportunities to play soccer with their peers because of the perceived "liability" for injuries. While it is true that including players with special needs in a fast-paced, combative environment like soccer demands more adaptation and improvisation than wheelchair basketball, students deserve the opportunity to participate. Teachers who facilitate a safe and competitive environment for students to play invasive sports like soccer truly provide a "least restrictive environment" for their students, which is required by federal law.

Note that many of the adaptive strategies and improvised equipment included for soccer are also applicable for field hockey, floor hockey, and lacrosse.

ADAPTING THE ENVIRONMENT AND TASK

Cognitive Adaptations

1. ***Boundary highlights.*** Use cones to help students distinguish the center-line, end-lines, sidelines, and goalie box. Recognition of these areas is critical to game-play.
2. ***Crowding rule.*** Explain that no more than two students may oppose each other for possession of the ball. Once the odds are two-against-one, the ball is awarded to the outnumbered player. Students will quickly learn not to "crowd" around the ball, and will be more willing to play their positions, pass, and take shots on goal.
3. ***Zone game play.*** Define each team in terms of "offensive" (shooting) players and "defensive" (capturing) players. Before the whistle sounds to begin game play, arrange each side of the field with an equal number of offensive and defensive players. Do not allow players to cross the centerline of the field during game play. This creates two separate zones, one on each side of the centerline. Opponents within each zone should be ability grouped for competitive equity.
4. ***Visual and manipulative scoring.*** Most people can not keep the running score for a game in their head. Once a ball is scored, it should be kept nearby the goal in which it was scored. Students will recognize the score by the number of balls in the respective net area.

5. **Trinity.** Provide the verbal cues, "pass," dribble," or "shoot" to students with the ball. The excitement of the game will leave some students unable to make quick decisions, which will frustrate teammates.
6. **Color coding.** Opponents need to wear different color jerseys. The goals should be color coded to remind students into which goal to shoot. Tying a jersey to the netting works well for this purpose.
7. **Whistle officiating.** Sound a whistle to stop game-play for officiating, as well as instruction during "teachable moments."

Affective Adaptations

1. **Kick-off circle.** Students with emotional challenges do not tolerate defensive pressure well. Require the defensive players to wait outside of the center circle until the ball travels outside of the circle lines. This affords an anxious player a stress-free start of the game.
2. **Goalie box.** Establish a goalie box boundary that offensive players may not enter. This provides a "cushion" of space between shooting players and defensive players-especially the goalie.
3. **Ability group teams.** Avoid traditional "team-captain" selection of teams. Inevitably the same students will consistently be picked last. Instead, adopt the routine of "ability grouping." This technique involves allowing students to pair themselves with a player of comparable ability. The partners then select opposite color jerseys and move to their respective areas. Teams will then be automatically "even" in terms of ability. In the case of an uneven number of students, the single player should partner with staff. This means that the staff person will need to be actively engaged in game play. If there is only one teacher, the single student may consider rotating into game play with a group of three.
4. **Goal-tending lacrosse and hockey.** Many programs do not have the appropriate safety equipment to protect goalies from injury during unrestricted game-play. Consider the rule that lacrosse balls shot on goal must bounce before entering the goal to be legal. In the same way, hockey pucks, too, must enter the goal below the goalie's knees to be legal.
5. **Modified balls/pucks for hockey and lacrosse.** Many programs do not provide goalies and players with safety gear like pads, gloves, and helmets. Softer, lighter options of lacrosse balls and hockey pucks are available commercially. For lacrosse, tennis balls are an inexpensive alternative to the regulation hard-rubber variety.

Sensorimotor Adaptations

1. **Beeper balls.** Beeper balls are usually made of foam and have an electronic beeping mechanism inserted into a cylinder shaped cavity. When the beeper is activated, it sounds a repetitive tone that visually impaired students use to track and locate balls. Beeper balls work well as hot balls during inclusive game play.
2. **Nerf balls.** Students who are visually impaired are vulnerable to being struck by equipment during class. Teacher judgment is critical to minimize the risk of regulation soccer balls striking visually impaired students. Nerf balls should be used during inclusive activities to minimize the risk of injury.
3. **Flat rubber discs.** Flat rubber discs may be placed on the floor or field to create a type of "Braille" crease boundary. Hence, visually impaired students may choose the crease option for inclusive game-play.
4. **Safety buddy.** A buddy may be assigned to protect visually impaired students from being struck by airborne balls.
5. **Scoring.** Score should be shown visually and called verbally to assist students with hearing and vision impairments.

IMPROVISING EQUIPMENT

As discussed in Part I, psychomotor modifications occur through the process of improvising the equipment and facility. The following modifications are introduced relative to three categories of equipment-traditional, alternative, and fabricated.

Traditional Equipment

1. **Soccer ball sizes and weights.** Soccer balls are available in "oversized" and "underweight" varieties. The best "trainer" balls are twice the size of the regulation soccer ball. Many simply have a leather cover over a latex balloon bladder.
2. **Lacrosse balls and hockey pucks.** For recreational programs that do not provide safety equipment and expert coaching, softer and lighter is better regarding lacrosse balls and hockey pucks. A wide variety are available commercially from sporting goods retailers.
3. **Soccer ball texture.** Rubber soccer balls provide durability, water-resistance, and maintain a "grippy" texture longer than leather soccer balls. Leather balls are preferred by students who want "regulation" game play.
4. **Nerf balls.** While limited in their bounce qualities, Nerf balls are invaluable as safe alternatives when including students who are anxious and or vulnerable to injury by regulation soccer balls.
5. **Geodesic mesh balls.** Geodesic balls are round and hollow, surrounded by molded cord in a mesh-like pattern. Students with spastic fingers can hold onto the mesh easily. Releasing is often successful by simply shaking or flinging the hand.
6. **Multicolored playground balls.** Students that have limited mobility spend the majority of their class time chasing soccer balls that roll away from them. Playground balls may be partially deflated such that they keep their round "ball" quality, needed for game play, but they flatten after hitting the floor, which limits the distance they roll away from the student.
7. **Standard soccer nets are usually width and height adjustable.** These may be set at varying widths and heights to accommodate students of different abilities. If the offensive players are not successful shooting past a goalie, consider making the goal area smaller and restricting the goalie from using his or her hands to block shots.
8. **Line machines.** Lines on grass fields may be either chalked or painted. A little preparation of the playing area will go a long way to helping students understand zones, positions, and boundaries.

Alternative Equipment

1. **Scooters.** Scooters equalize. That is, able-bodied students who sit on scooters are often disadvantaged by height and mobility such that students using wheelchairs, canes, and walkers can be competitive. It is interesting to observe an inclusive game where all able-bodied players struggle with the frustration of being scooter-disabled. It is equally interesting to observe the student using a wheelchair in a position of dominance and control. If hands are used instead of feet, soccer, in effect, becomes "handball." Handball is an excellent lead-up activity, preparatory activity, inclusive activity, and or "rainy day" alternative.
2. **Electric leaf blower or vacuum** (reversed airflow). Use the blower to send balloons, beach balls, or soccer balls across the field-indoors or outdoors.
3. **Wheelchairs.** Able-bodied students may elect to participate in an inclusive game of wheelchair handball. Note that handball is the same game as soccer-but with hands. As with scooters, the experience will facilitate an awareness of the challenges associated with a disabling condition.

4. ***Cage balls.*** Cage balls are oversized inflatable balls that are often multi-colored. Some come as large as 72 inches in diameter. Cage balls may be used in a variety of individual activities involving pushing the ball into a variety of goals. This type of "giant soccer ball" is tailormade for Kevin, who can use his chair to safely push the ball.

5. ***Shuffle cues and Velcro.*** Shuffle cues provide safe, lightweight, poles for extending the reach of students-particularly for hockey and soccer. When Velcro is attached to the tip, the extended pole takes on grasp and release properties. A student using a wheelchair may use the "pole," with Velcro, to grab a lightweight ball or puck and maneuver it toward a goal. Shuffle cues are particularly effective as adaptive hockey sticks, in which students may push pucks with greater success. Teachers may incorporate this skill into a variety of individual, preparatory, and inclusive activities.

6. ***Lacrosse sticks and Velcro.*** Velcro may be placed on the outer part of the lacrosse stick head such that students may pick up Velcro balls. Many types of Velcro will "grab" tennis balls, which are great for lacrosse activities. Once the ball is attached to the stick, it may be raised by the student, and manually placed in the pocket of the stick for passing, cradling, or shooting.

Fabricated Equipment

1. ***The claw.*** See Part I for description. The claw was designed specifically for wheelchairs for use during Soccer activities. The benefit of using the claw device is that students may maneuver regulation Soccer gameballs for passing, dribbling, or shooting, in a fully inclusive game-without using hands! Games including wheelchairs with a mounted claw require safety rules related to offensive and defensive interactions with the player using the claw. The player using the claw chooses to be a hot, crease, or clock player. This limits the need for physical contact with able-bodied players.

2. ***PVC chute.*** See Part I for description. The chute provides a student-controlled path along which balls may reach a designated goal. The chute may be used to send balls to a partner or opponent.

3. ***Catapult.*** See Part I for description. The catapult allows students to mechanically launch balls toward a designated goal with minimal physical effort.

4. ***The Arch.*** The arch may be used as a concrete spatial reference as a goal for shooting or a boundary for passing. Tetherballs may also be suspended from the arch to provide kicking and trapping practice.

IPI INCLUSION MODEL

Individual Activities

Soccer may be thought of as a thematic game involving working as part of a team to put an object into a designated goal. Keeping this loose framework in mind, we develop activities that allow students to participate in activities that they can master individually, at their developmental levels. Students who master these activities may choose to participate in more advanced and "game-like" preparatory activities. Get out of your box and keep an open mind! Students love these activities.

1. ***Catapult soccer.*** Position the catapult such that a student can drop a soccer ball onto the raised arm of the lever. Position the fulcrum so the catapulted object (tennis balls work well) is launched toward a goal. The catapulted object may be launched toward targets on the wall or into containers resting on the floor.

2. ***Chute soccer.*** (Resembles a bowling lane gutter) The chute is used as a means of providing force and momentum to a ball by a student that is severely disabled. One end of the chute

would balance between the student's knees while seated, rest on a raised stationary object, or could be held with one hand. The ball that is placed at the raised end will roll along the chute toward a designated goal.

3. *Pulley volleyball.* Attach one end of the tether cord to a ball. The student holds onto the other end. Throw the tether cord over a basketball rim (or some other object positioned over a volleyball net) so it glides over the top in a pulley fashion. As the student pulls the tether cord, the ball will raise, lower, and swing. Games may be created that involve dropping the ball into a designated position or container. The tether cord may be attached to electric wheelchairs if the student is unable to manually hold or manipulate it.

4. *Air hose soccer.* Use an electric leaf blower, or the blower option on a vacuum, to blow balloons or lightweight balls toward a goal.

5. *Pole soccer.* Use the shuffle cue to lift or push balls toward goal. Velcro may be used to grasp and release balls. The ball will need to be banged or rubbed to remove it from the Velcro. A clothespin may be attached to the pole near the student's hand, fixed such that it pinches a string to the pole. The string runs along the shaft, like on a fishing pole, and has a ball tied to its end. When the student presses the clothespin, the string is released and the ball drops.

6. *Foosball.* Foosball is an excellent individual soccer activity for students with disabilities. Many students will likely express interest in playing foosball, since it is arcade-like. This provides a means for partnering peer teachers, as well as untrained classmates.

7. *Air hockey.* Air hockey tables work equally as well as foosball tables as Individual activities.

Preparatory Activities

By definition, the nature of these activities prepares students for participation in the inclusive activity. Therefore, any activity that prepares a student for participation with the main body of the class may be considered preparatory. Students typically need practice selecting which primary competitive adaptation is best for them. They also need practice with small groups of peers at this level of participation.

1. *Hot ball practice.* The student gains familiarity with his or her selected ball by receiving, trapping, catching, carrying, dribbling, and or shooting, individually.

2. *Crease practice* (trinity). The student works with a partner or small group to practice passing and receiving passes within his or her identified crease space. Emphasis should be placed on trapping without losing the ball, passing to a partner, and shooting the ball toward a goal.

3. *Clock practice* (partner/small group). The student works with a partner or small group to practice trapping, passing, receiving passes, and shooting-all within the designated countdown duration. Staff need to help the student identify a challenging duration, in seconds. The duration should be less than 10 seconds before the student participates with the main body of the class.

Note: Students with special needs may choose to practice the general concepts of the game by playing handball. This game uses the same rules, boundaries, and concepts as soccer, except students throw and catch using their hands.

Inclusive Activities
Recreational

1. *Handball.* An indoor or outdoor soccer-like activity, except hands are used to throw and catch a Nerf-type ball.

2. ***Ghostbusters.*** Each student places a bowling pin (ghost) on the floor, and uses his or her feet to protect the pin from being knocked down by soccer balls. Nerf-type soccer balls are positioned all over the gym floor. Students choose the best time to leave their pins unprotected so they may kick a ball toward another player's pin. If a player's pin is knocked down (busted) then the player needs to execute a designated number of exercises to "re-energize" their "ghost," (reset their pin). The game ends after a set duration of time.

3. ***Dribble tag.*** Students are positioned randomly around the gym or field. A select few students or staff members wear jerseys and are the "taggers." Each student dribbles his or her soccer ball away from the taggers. Once a "tagger" touches a player's soccerball with his or her foot, the player stands frozen with wide legs. A friend must dribble close and shoot a soccer ball between the frozen player's legs to unfreeze him or her. Students with special needs may kick hot balls toward classmates to freeze them. They may also carry a hot stick with which to touch freeze players. Students with wheelchairs may be fully included as taggers or dribblers, especially if they use the claw.

4. ***Scooter handball.*** The student using a wheelchair, cane, or walker maintains the advantage of height and mobility in this game because able-bodied peers play while sitting on scooters. All rules for a small group-game of soccer apply. The adaptation is the restricted mobility and height of the scooters for the able-bodied players.

5. ***Wheelchair soccer.*** Able-bodied players use wheelchairs to play against their peers who are skilled and practiced at using the claw device attached to their wheelchairs.

Lead-up Activities

1. ***Capture soccer.*** (Confronting the opponent). The playing area is separated into three equally spaced zones. Students start in zone 1, where they select soccer ball from a barrel. Zone 2 contains two-four players wearing jerseys who are designated defensive capturers. The capturers are instructed how to safely intercept the ball from the offensive players in Zone 1. The object of the game is for each player in Zone 1 to dribble his or her soccer ball past the capturing players in Zone 2 so that they can reach the safety of Zone 3. Once in Zone 3, students shoot until they score a goal. After a goal is scored, the ball is placed in a container, and students return to Zone 1 to get a new soccer ball and repeat the cycle. If a soccer ball is captured, both the ball and the offensive player return to Zone 1 to try again. Students using wheelchairs, canes, or walkers may participate in either the offensive or capturing roles.

2. ***Trash ball.*** (Clean out the backyard). This game is simple, yet students of all ages and abilities enjoy it. Position one team on each side of the centerline, and flood the gymnasium floor with soft soccer balls. Students are directed to kick soccer balls across the center-line and onto their opponents' side of the field. Add music, and stop all play when the music stops. A quick survey of the floor will tell which team is kicking more balls than the other. Restart the music and cue students as required.

3. ***Scatter.*** Two teams are ability-grouped, wear opposite color jerseys, and are positioned on opposite sides of the centerline. Students are allowed to cross the centerline. The teacher dumps a variety of soft balls in the center of the field (there should be more balls than students) which starts the activity. Students shoot soccer balls into their respective goal (on their side). Soccer balls that enter the goal are collected in a container. Once all balls have been scored, each team counts their score. The game may be repeated as required.

4. ***Keep away soccer.*** This is an extension of scatter. One player from each team is allowed to cross the centerline into their opponent's side during the scatter activity. This single player acts alone to defend the goal and kick soccer balls to his or her team. Players may be added to each side, and the number of balls may be reduced, until the activity becomes a soccer game-with equal numbers of shooters and capturers on each side of the centerline.

PRIMARY COMPETITIVE ADAPTATIONS

1. *Hot ball player.* Players choosing a hot ball may receive, pass, and shoot balls within the competitive milieu of the class. This adaptation provides game-like stimulation for students with special needs who are not ready for fully inclusive play.
2. *Crease-player.* Players choosing to be assigned a crease area pass, receive, and shoot in a static zone where other players are restricted. This affords a student with special needs the opportunity to incorporate closed skills into an open skill environment. Soccer creases work best when they are positioned parallel to the sidelines of the field or gym.
3. *Clock player.* Students choosing to be a clock player in soccer should be able to execute the trinity in ten seconds or less. More than ten seconds delays the game and increases player frustration. This option should be used when a player's skills will not permit him or her to dribble, pass, or shoot without losing possession of the ball to an opponent. This adaptation takes practice and patience by all players, and is best with the support of at least one engaged staff person.

PROGRESSIVE COMPETITIVE LEVELS SPORT SEQUENCE

Purpose: To provide structure to the positions and control to the pacing of the game.
 # Players: 4-12 players per team, two teams
Equipment: One regulation or adapted soccer ball.
Two soccer goals positioned opposite each other.
Field boundaries highlighted with cones or flat discs.
Clearly marked centerline.
Colored jerseys for each team.
Scoring containers positioned at each goal.
At least one engaged staff member.

Note: Students with special needs may participate using an inclusive activity at any progressive competitive level (PCL).

7-Level Soccer

Description: Students are in two teams of ability-grouped students. Each team is positioned on their respective side of the center line. The adaptations that follow involve modifications of the required skills (task), and both the field area and rules (environment). Students who are expected to participate in competitive soccer activities should begin by playing level 1 soccer. Once the majority of the students in the group have demonstrated mastery at level 1, they should be allowed to transition to level 2 play.

Students who have not mastered the skills for a particular level should be allowed to participate in a game with peers at the same ability level. Students who are ready to progress to the next competitive level should participate with peers of the same ability. It is common to have several games being played at the same time; each game meets the developmental needs of students. For example, in any given class, Terrell may play a game of level 3 soccer, while Maggie plays at level 5. Students may demonstrate mastery of level 1 or level 2 skills in a few minutes. The teacher should allow the students to progress when they demonstrate readiness, or the students will become frustrated and lose interest. In my experience, most intermediate classes (grades three to five) progress through levels 1 and 2 in the introductory lesson. Most will progress through levels 3 and 4 during the second lesson. Ultimately, the majority of the students will reach their competitive limit at levels 4 or 5. By the conclusion of a soccer unit, a select few students play at levels 1, 2, or 3. The majority of the students play at levels 4 or 5, while some advanced players compete at levels 6 or 7. If the teacher develops the criteria for progressive levels appropriately, student performance should fit the standard bell curve parameters.

Level 1: Mass Soccer (Trashball)

1. Position one team on each side of the center-line, and flood the gymnasium floor with soft soccer balls.
2. Students are directed to kick soccer balls across the center-line and onto their opponents' side of the field.
3. Add music, and stop all play when the music stops.
4. A quick survey of the floor will tell which team is kicking more balls than the other.
5. Re-start the music and cue students as required.

Level 2: Scatter Soccer

1. Two ability-grouped teams are positioned opposite the centerline on a field or gymnasium. Students wear color-coded jerseys.
2. An engaged staff member dumps soccer balls in the center of the playing area, which signals the start of the game.
3. Players may cross the centerline at this level.
4. Players dribble and shoot soccer balls into their respective goal. Scored balls remain in the goal, or are positioned in a scoring container.
5. The round ends when all balls are scored. Each team counts their respective score.
6. The game may be replayed when all balls are returned to the center area.

Level 3: Capture Soccer

1. All rules for level 2 apply except:
2. Students may not cross the centerline.
3. One player, (the capturer) or (defense-player), is positioned on the side of the field with the opposing shooters. Their should be several offensive shooters and only one defender.
4. The capturing player is not a goalie. The capturing player intercepts soccer balls from the shooters and kicks them to his or her shooting team across the centerline.
5. The game ends when all soccer balls are scored.
6. The capturer rejoins his or her team to count the scored soccer balls.
7. When a new round begins, the capturer may designate a teammate to be the next capturing player.

Level 4: Goalie Soccer

1. All rules for level 3 apply except:
2. A second defensive player is added-a goal tender.
3. The goal tender and the capturer work together to keep the shooters from scoring.
4. The goalie has a special zone, the goal box, in which no shooters may enter.
5. The goalie may also use his or her hands to block soccer balls. The type of ball, size of goal, and size of goal box should reflect the ability of the students. Think safety!

Level 5: 3-Ball Zone Soccer

1. All rules for level 4 apply except:
2. An equal number of shooters and capturers (offensive and defensive players) should be positioned on each side of the centerline. A typical arrangement is four offensive players versus four defensive players per side. Players may not cross the centerline at this level.
3. Each offensive-defensive group is restricted to their respective side of the field. When the ball travels across the centerline, the next group gains possession.
4. An engaged staff person should "trickle" a second ball into the game, if the action "slows," provide more "time-on-task" and reduce "wait-time."
5. If the score becomes 2-0, the winning team shakes hands with the losing team, and the game re-starts. If the score becomes 1-1, the third ball is put into play as the tie-breaking ball.

6. This 3 ball concept is critical in that it provides many brief games which:
A. Engages students with short attention spans
B. Keeps the games "low stakes" which decreases "loss anxiety"
C. Reinforces scorekeeping, and facilitates "teachable moments"
D. Reinforces sportsmanship
E. Provides for rests and water breaks
F. Allows changes of players and position

Level 6: Forward Soccer
1. All rules for level 5 apply except:
2. One player is designated a "forward" player, and allowed to cross the centerline to play from goal to goal.
3. The 3-ball concept may still be developmentally appropriate. Use as required per student readiness.

Level 7: Regulation Soccer
1. Regulation game play.
2. At least one engaged staff person is recommended. Engaged staff should be officials or player-officials. Remember! Students need constant constructive feedback during game play.

Case Studies

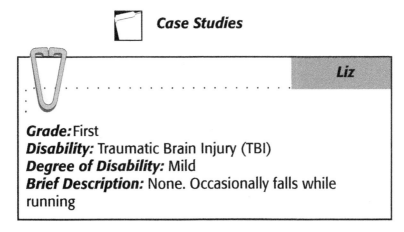

Grade: First
Disability: Traumatic Brain Injury (TBI)
Degree of Disability: Mild
Brief Description: None. Occasionally falls while running

Liz

Soccer Participation:
Liz enjoys being outside for soccer activities. She especially likes playing on the grass field, because it hurts less when she falls. Liz also works with the students who use wheelchairs. A few students have electric chairs which move well on the grass field. Some students have manual wheelchairs, which are maneuvered easiest on the asphalt court surface.

Her favorite individual activity includes using a wheelchair fitted with a claw to push a soccer ball around. She is a good role model for students who can not play without their wheelchairs.

During preparatory activities, Liz practices trapping moving soccer balls. This is the skill she needs to work on most for gameplay. Liz practices in a group of three students. They take turns passing, trapping, and shooting at the goal.

During inclusive lead-ups, Liz enjoys taking the ball from her classmates during capture soccer. She also likes to knock over her classmates' pins during the ghostbusters activity. Dribble tag is frustrating for Liz with a regulation soccer ball until the teacher partially deflated it to limit its roll-ability.

Liz participates fully in the soccer games in class. By the end of the unit, Liz is successful playing as a capturing player during level 3 soccer.

Kevin

Grade: Fourth
Disability: Orthopedic Impairment (OI), Cerebral Palsy
Degree of Disability: Severe and profound
Brief Description: Paralysis from the neck down. Learning to control spastic movement initiated from left shoulder to manipulate the joystick control on his electric wheelchair.

Soccer Participation:

The soccer claw was made for students like Kevin. This device allows Kevin to participate at all three levels-individual, preparatory, and inclusive. He spends his first few lessons practicing how to maneuver his chair to control the soccer ball.

The teacher transitions between the main body of the class and Kevin to provide feedback and praise. After the second lesson, the teacher introduces a preparatory skill that Kevin may use during gameplay. It involves using his electric wheelchair to maneuver (dribble) a hot ball on the asphalt court through a PVC arch to score a goal. Kevin practices this while a small group of peers played a game on the same court. The gameplay and action around him makes it difficult for him to focus on driving his chair. This is the very skill that he will need to participate inclusively.

Kevin uses the claw to maneuver the soccer ball around players, out of corners, and through the arch uprights. He also practices stopping rolling balls and changing direction while dribbling. Any skill, drill, or lead-up in which his peers participated, Kevin can participate-only with a hot ball and at a slower pace.

By the end of the unit, Kevin participates in an inclusive soccer game on the court using his hot ball. Each time he scores the ball through the uprights of the arch, his team scores a point. During a ten-minute game, Kevin scores an average of two points. As Kevin's skills improve, the inclusive rules will need to change to keep the game fair. He will likely be able to work toward being a crease player, and ultimately a clock player.

Maggie

Grade: Seventh
Disability: Orthopedic Impairment (OI), Cerebral Palsy
Degree of Disability: Moderate
Brief Description: Paraplegia affecting both legs, but not arms. Uses a wheelchair, walker, and/or quad canes, depending on the activity.

Soccer Participation:

Maggie chooses to skip the activities at the individual level and begin her work at the preparatory level. She excels at the warm-up games like Capture soccer. Maggie uses her manual wheelchair on the court with the Claw during the beginning of each class. She knows this allows the teacher time to organize the main body of the class.

Maggie tries all of the primary competitive adaptations during preparatory activities, and chooses to be a crease player, using her quad canes for her first inclusive game. Maggie enjoys receiving the ball in the crease, but finds it difficult to score from the side of the field. The following class she played as a clock player, and finds that to be more fun. She plays well, positioning herself in front of the goal to receive passes. Once she touches the ball, she earnes five seconds to execute a dribble, pass, or shot. She frequently takes shots, and scores at least once per game.

By the end of the unit, Maggie plays with her peers as a clock player for at least one game during the class. Using her canes on the grass is physically demanding. Maggie rests while using the claw during individual activities on the asphalt court area adjacent to the field.

Phil

Grade: Eleventh
Disability: Orthopedic Impairment (OI), Below Knee Amputee
Degree of Disability: Moderate
Brief Description: Phil is learning to use his newly fitted prosthesis, and chooses to use his wheelchair depending on the activity. He is athletic and competitive.

Soccer Participation:

Phil spends the first half of class participating with his prosthesis, and the second half using his wheelchair. This gives his leg a much-needed chance to rest and recover from the workout. During warm-ups, Phil takes his time and walks through the activities. Phil chooses to play competitively, on the grass field, and does not like to use the primary competitive adaptations. His peers do not offer him any special privileges or favors, but he accommodates with good positioning and making immediate passes or shots on goal. When Phil transitions to his chair, he officiates competitive games. Phil also spends a part of each class working at the Preparatory level, practicing trapping and shooting. Phil's limited mobility has forced him to develop into one of the most accurate shooters in the program. Even so, he still participates at level 5 soccer-the highest level in the class.

Chart 8-1:
Soccer Activities by Degree of Disability

	Mild	Moderate	Severe
Individual			
Catapult Soccer		X	X
Chute Soccer		X	X
Pulley Soccer		X	X
Air Hose Soccer		X	X
Pole Soccer		X	X
Foosball		X	X
Air Hockey			
Preparatory			
Hot Ball Practice	X	X	X
Crease Practice	X	X	X
Clock Practice	X	X	X
Inclusive			
Handball	X	X	X
Ghostbusters	X	X	X
Dribble Tag	X	X	X
Scooter Handball	X	X	X
Wheelchair Soccer	X	X	X
Capture Soccer	X	X	X
Trashball Soccer	X	X	X
Scatter Soccer	X	X	X
Keep Away Soccer	X	X	X
PCL Levels 1-7	X	X	X

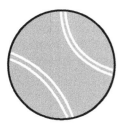

CHAPTER 9

Tennis

Most gymnasiums and outdoor courts are designed to accommodate tennis activities. The implication is that tennis, and tennis-like activities, are both popular and accessible. Tennis may be practiced individually, using a wall for rebound-play, or played with partners and small groups. It requires a net, a few tennis balls and one racquet per player.

Students who have not received proper instruction and practice typically have difficulty with tennis. It is not an activity that comes naturally to most, and competitive game-play includes challenging rules and scoring. For many students, simply rallying a ball back and forth over the net becomes frustrating after a short time. Participation in tennis activities requires a developmentally appropriate skill progression, adapted rules and scoring, and improvised equipment. Teaching tennis is a programmatic reality check. Students will either be successful and motivated in the first few sessions, or they will become frustrated, act-out behaviorally, and or just quit. This chapter, more than any other, was born of trial and error with what works and what does not-with students with or without disabilities.

ADAPTING THE ENVIRONMENT AND TASK

Cognitive Adaptations
1. **Court numbers.** Each court needs a number or letter such that students can identify a specific area of play.
2. **Boundary highlights.** Use cones or brightly colored tape to help students distinguish the court lines from the various other lines on the floor.
3. **Electric fence.** Students will associate electricity with, "Do not touch," which helps them remember net rules.
4. **Line rule.** Explain that the ball may bounce inside the lines or on the lines for game play to continue.
5. **Bounce rule.** Explain that the ball may only bounce once before it returned over the net.
6. **Net rule.** Explain that the ball must go over the net for game-play to continue.
7. **Calling the score.** Most people can not keep the running score for a game in their head. Tennis, like other net activities, provides for frequent verbal reminders of the score. Each server should be required to verbally call the score before each serve. Failure to call the score should result in a point awarded the opponent.
8. **Soft touch serving concept.** Students should practice rallying balls under the arch (see improvised equipment section) to help them understand the "soft" swing necessary to keep the ball within court boundaries. Verbal directions to "swing easier," mean little to a

student who requires concrete and or visual feedback. The arch makes success or failure concrete. Tennis balls travelling under the arch are more likely to remain within the court boundaries.

9. **Score translation.** Students should initially learn to keep score in tennis using zero, one, two, three, and four. Students may later be introduced to regulation tennis scoring terms using the score translation chart. The chart should be posted so students may refer to it during game play.

Diagram 9-1
Tennis Score Translation Chart

Beginner	0	1	2	3	4 (Game Over)
Advanced	Love	15	30	40	Game Over

10. **Advantage-in / Advantage-out floor model.** This model is critical for teaching students with limited cognition to understand the abstract concepts associated with advantage-scoring. Two students should physically stand on the deuce mats positioned evenly across to symbolize the "tie" score. When one student wins the next point, he or she moves one position forward toward the "win" mat, while the opponent moves one position backward toward the "lose" mat. The server may then read the mat under his or her feet which reflects the correct score-ad-in or ad-out respectively. Should the score return to deuce, students stand even with each other. Only after a student earns two consecutive points does he or she stand on the winner's mat. The model should be readily available during game play for reference as required by students.

Diagram 9-2
Advantage-In/Out Floor Model

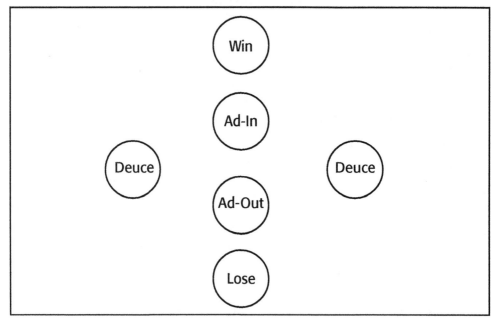

11. *Walking the boundaries.* Students should walk the boundaries of their court to demonstrate clear spatial understanding.

Affective Adaptations

1. *Choice serving.* Students with emotional challenges do not tolerate serving failure well. Offer students the opportunity to choose the distance from the net for their serve. Encourage underhand serving for greater control.
2. *Court courtesy.* One of the causes for fights and arguments in tennis is students running through other players' courts to retrieve tennis balls. Demonstrate waiting for the other players to return the ball or walking around a court to retrieve a ball. Praise students who demonstrate court courtesy.
3. *Ability group partners.* This technique involves allowing students to pair themselves with a player of comparable ability.
4. *Rotation players.* Allow players to decide if they want to rotate to other courts to play other partners. Some players will choose to remain with the same partner throughout the activity. This should be permitted as long as the students remain on task and play cooperatively.
5. *Server/receiver choice.* Some students will prefer to play a competitive game as only the server or only the receiver-depending on skill mastery. This should be permitted as long as the opponent accepts the other position.

Sensorimotor Adaptations

1. *Beeper balls.* Beeper balls are usually made of foam and have an electronic beeping mechanism inserted into a cylinder-shaped cavity. When the beeper is activated, it sounds a repetitive tone that visually-impaired students use to track and locate balls. Beeper balls work well as hot balls during inclusive game play.
2. *Foam tennis balls.* Students who are visually impaired are vulnerable to being struck by equipment during class-particularly tennis balls. Teacher judgment is critical to minimize the risk of regulation tennis balls striking visually impaired students. Foam tennis balls should be used during inclusive activities to minimize the risk of injury.
3. *Flat rubber discs.* Flat rubber discs may be placed on the floor to create a type of "Braille" boundary.
4. *The grab-and-toss.* Visually impaired students are allowed to grab the net, to gain spatial perspective, before they serve or return the ball over the net.
5. *Safety buddy.* A buddy may be assigned to protect visually impaired students from being struck by airborne balls.
6. *Scoring.* Score should be shown visually and called verbally to assist students with hearing and vision impairments.

IMPROVISING EQUIPMENT

As discussed in Part I, psychomotor modifications occur through the process of improvising the equipment and facility. The following modifications are introduced relative to three categories of equipment-traditional, alternative, and fabricated.

Traditional Equipment

1. *Tennis balls.* Tennis balls are available in a variety of weights, materials, and sizes. Plastic wiffle balls are used for small-court pickleball, foam tennis balls are best for indoor play, and regulation tennis balls work well outdoors. Other balls that are suitable for tennis striking include balloons, beach balls, and five-inch playground balls.

2. ***Tennis ball elasticity (bounce factor).*** One of the great challenges for teachers is to include a ball that provides the correct bounce-action for the space and ability level of the players. Regulation tennis balls used indoors with multiple courts usually have too much bounce for students. It is difficult to hit the ball softly enough to keep it in the court. Foam tennis balls are available commercially with a variety of densities for variable "bounciness." Foam tennis balls provide surprisingly real "action" from the racquet and do not hurt if a ball hits another student.

3. ***Racquets.*** For the beginner, the best racquet is the hand! From a motor-skill perspective, the farther the ball is from the hand and arm at contact, the more difficult it is to hit with control. Students should start hitting playground balls with their hand-preferably through the arch for spatial awareness. Students who master hitting with their hand should earn a pickleball paddle. Pickleball paddles look like oversized table-tennis paddles, and work best when used with plastic wiffle balls. The next best racquet would be a racquetball racquet. Once students demonstrate mastery with the racquetball racquet, they may progress to a regulation tennis racquet.

4. ***Geodesic mesh balls.*** Geodesic balls are round and hollow, surrounded by molded cord in a mesh-like pattern. Students with spastic fingers can hold onto the mesh easily. Releasing is often successful by simply shaking or flinging the hand.

5. ***Multicolored playground balls.*** Students that have limited mobility spend the majority of their class time chasing tennis balls that roll away from them. Playground balls may be partially deflated such that they keep their round "ball" quality, needed for game-play, but they flatten after hitting the floor, which limits the distance they roll away from the student.

6. ***Standard tennis nets are usually height adjustable.*** These may be set at varying heights to accommodate students of different abilities. It is often desirable to allow the net to sag in the center, providing a less-challenging area for students with limited tossing or hitting abilities.

Alternative Equipment

1. ***Mat craters*** (Tumbling mats stood on edges and curved to form crater-like areas). These craters provide students a container for which to serve foam tennis balls. One or more students may position themselves inside the mat crater to repel or toss out balls as they enter. This is a particularly stimulating space for students in wheelchairs, as they are likely to be bombarded with incoming tennis balls.

2. ***Scooters.*** Scooters equalize. That is, able-bodied students that sit on scooters are often disadvantaged by height and mobility such that students using wheelchairs, canes, and walkers can be competitive. It is interesting to observe an inclusive game where all able-bodied players struggle with the frustration of being scooter-disabled. It is equally interesting to observe the student using a wheelchair in a position of dominance and control.

3. ***Electric leaf blower or vacuum*** (reversed airflow). Use the blower to send balloons, beach balls, or soap bubbles over the net.

4. ***Wheelchairs.*** Able-bodied students may elect to participate in an inclusive game of wheelchair tennis. As with scooters, the experience will facilitate an awareness of the challenges associated with a disabling condition.

5. ***Cage balls.*** Cage balls are oversized inflatable balls that are often multi-colored. Some come as large as 72 inches in diameter. Consider a cooperative tennis game in which a small group needed to work together to balance the giant ball on a dixie cup. Cage balls may be used in a variety of individual activities involving pushing the ball up and over the net.

6. ***Beach balls.*** Beach balls are lightweight, colorful, and have a special feature which few teachers utilize-the inflation stem. When pulled outward, the stem provides a handy appendage from which students can pick up, carry, and release. This is particularly helpful

for students who are limited in their ability to reach from their wheelchair, cane, or walker. The stem is also helpful for underhand serving. Students hold the ball by the stem with one hand, and strike with the other.

7. *Parachute.* It is unfortunate that parachutes are frequently limited to early childhood and young children in most programs. The parachute is one of the most popular alternative pieces of sports equipment among middle and high school students in our programs. The parachute may be used by groups of students to launch tennis balls up and over the net.

8. *Shuffle cues and Velcro.* Shuffle cues provide safe, lightweight, poles for extending the reach of students. When Velcro is attached to the tip, the extended pole takes on gasp and release properties. A student using a wheelchair may use the "pole," with Velcro, to grab a lightweight ball from the floor, lift it over the net, and bang it such that the ball falls into the opponents court. Teachers may incorporate this skill into a variety of individual, preparatory, and inclusive activities.

9. *Table tennis.* Table tennis provides an alternative activity for students during the tennis unit.

10. *Video tennis (Pong).* One of the first video games made for home use was Pong, a tennis-like game. Students with limited mobility, and even major paralysis, may play Tennis-like activities electronically by manipulating a video joystick.

11. *Electric ball machines.* Tennis ball machines launch tennis balls (like a baseball pitching machine) in a variety of trajectories and speeds. Students who are anxious about other tennis activities may be motivated to participate using the ball machine.

Fabricated Equipment

1. *PVC chute.* See Part I for description. The chute provides a student-controlled path along which balls may reach a designated goal. The chute may be used with a low net to send balls to a partner or opponent.

2. *Catapult.* See Part I for description. The catapult allows students to mechanically launch balls over the net with minimal physical effort.

3. *The arch.* The arch may be used as a concrete spatial reference that communicates boundaries for striking. Students may hit the ball under the arch or over the arch. Tetherballs may also be suspended from the arch to provide catching, tossing, and striking practice.

4. *The pole.* The teacher holds the pole, much like a fishing pole, with a lightweight ball attached to the pole by a length of cord. The teacher uses the pole to "hover" the ball in front of the student, making it easier to hit. The teacher may also use the pole to move the ball over the net following a hit by the student. This is particularly helpful when the student does not hit the ball with enough force to send it over the net.

IPI INCLUSION MODEL

Individual Activities

Tennis may be thought of as a thematic game involving striking an object over another object. Keeping this loose framework in mind, we develop activities that allow students to participate in activities that they can master individually, at their developmental levels. Students who master these activities may choose to participate in more advanced and "game-like" preparatory activities. Get out of your box and keep an open mind! Students love these activities.

1. *Catapult tennis.* Position the catapult such that a student can drop a heavy object (or strike using the head of a racquet) onto the raised arm of the lever. Position the fulcrum so the catapulted object (tennis balls work well) is launched over the net. The catapulted object may be launched toward targets on the wall, over regulation nets, or into containers resting on the floor.

2. **Chute tennis.** (Resembles a bowling lane gutter) The chute should be placed on a stack of mats such that it can pivot 360 degrees and tilt up and down. The chute may be positioned over a low net. The student holds one end of the chute and places a ball at the end nearest him or her. The student may tilt or pivot the chute as the ball rolls toward the opposite end. One objective may be to simply control the chute such that the ball drops over the net. Another objective may be to maneuver the chute so the ball drops into a designated area. A third objective may be to send the ball to a partner, who would return it along the chute. Tip: Use different types of balls to vary the speed with which it rolls along the chute. Tip: Mark the ends of the chute with colored tape for visual tracking.

3. **Pulley tennis.** Attach one end of the tether cord to a ball. The student holds onto the other end. Throw the tether cord over a basketball rim (or some other object positioned over a net) so it glides over the top in a pulley fashion. As the student pulls the tether cord, the ball will raise, lower, and swing. Games may be created that involve dropping the ball into a designated position or container. Advanced students may even pull the ball so that it moves up and over the net. The tether cord may be attached to electric wheelchairs if the student is unable to manually hold or manipulate it.

4. **Air hose tennis.** Use an electric leaf blower, or the blower option on a vacuum, to blow balloons or soap bubbles into the air and over the net.

5. **Pole tennis.** Use the shuffle cue to lift balls toward the net. Velcro may be used to grasp and release balls. The ball will need to be banged or rubbed to remove it from the Velcro. A clothespin may be attached to the pole near the student's hand, fixed such that it pinches a string to the pole. The string runs along the shaft, like on a fishing pole, and has a ball tied to its end. When the student presses the clothes pin, the string is released and the ball drops.

6. **Crater tennis.** This activity involves using a mat crater as a collection space for foam tennis balls that are hit or served into the crater. Students using assistive devices enjoy being selected as the students who are positioned inside the crater to receive and return the balls. Note that the incoming balls will likely strike the students inside the craters, which adds to the excitement of the activity. Use foam-type tennis balls for safety.

Preparatory Activities

By definition, the nature of these activities prepares students for participation in the inclusive activity. Therefore, any activity that prepares a student for participation with the main body of the class may be considered preparatory. Students typically need practice selecting which primary competitive adaptation is best for them. They also need practice with small groups of peers at this level of participation.

1. **Hot ball practice.** The student gains familiarity with his or her selected ball by catching, tossing, and/or striking it individually. Students may choose to practice with a teacher partner, a peer partner, or use the wall as a rebound partner. Students who play in tournaments may use the hot ball.

2. **Crease practice.** The student works with a partner to practice serving and receiving serves within his or her identified crease space. The crease space may be marked by cones, tape, or hoops. The crease space in tennis activities functions as a limited area into which partners must serve. In effect, it reduces the court size of the student with special needs.

3. **Clock practice.** The student works with a partner to practice serving and sending the ball over the net-all within the designated countdown duration. Staff need to help the student identify a challenging duration, in seconds. The duration should be less than 10 seconds before the student participates with the main body of the class.

Note: Students with special needs should play at a low net with a designated peer partner before entering an inclusive game. This will help them to understand the rules, as well as provide opportunities to practice their modified skills under "dynamic" game-play pressure.

Inclusive Activities
Recreational
1. **Parachute tennis.** Parachute tennis involves a group of si6-12 students who work together to fling the parachute upward such that tennis balls in the center are catapulted over the net. This also provides teachable moments for principles of physics-momentum, angles, force, acceleration, rebound, and trajectory.
2. **Scooter tennis.** The student using a wheelchair, cane, or walker maintains the advantage of height and mobility in this game because able-bodied peers play while sitting on scooters. All rules for tennis apply. The adaptation is the restricted mobility and height of the scooters for the able-bodied players.
3. **Wheelchair tennis.** Able-bodied players use wheelchairs to play against their peers who are skilled and practiced at using wheelchairs, canes, and walkers.

Lead-up Activities
1. **Keep it up.** Students use their hands or racquets to strike balls into the air (volley) repeatedly without allowing the ball to hit the ground. Students may count the number of times they volley the ball in the air. Encourage low, soft hits.
2. **Wall ball rally.** Students may practice hitting a tennis ball against a designated space on the wall such that it bounces once on the floor before it is returned to the wall. Teachers may establish a minimum number of hits before a student is eligible for game play.
3. **Trashball** (Clean out the backyard). This game is simple, yet students of all ages and abilities enjoy it. Position one team on each side of a net, and flood the gymnasium floor with foam tennis balls. Students are directed to serve into their opponents' court. Add music, and stop all play when the music stops. A quick survey of the floor will tell which team is hitting more balls than the other. Re-start the music and cue students as required.
4. **Mass tennis.** A large group of students is positioned facing a wall, such as the wall of a gymnasium. The teacher starts the game by tossing a Tennis ball against the wall. Students remain in their designated positions. When the ball rebounds close to a student, he or she may return it to the wall. The ball may be returned to the wall as long as it is hit on a bounce. The ball is dead when it rolls, and the game restarts. The object of the game is to keep the rally going as long as possible. Use position markers to help students play in their respective positions.
5. **Crater serving.** This activity involves small groups of students tasked with serving large numbers of foam tennis balls into their respective craters. Students using wheelchairs, canes, or walkers may position themselves inside the crater. Their objective is to collect and toss out the tennis balls faster than their peers can serve them in. Students with special needs may also elect to be the shooting players.

PRIMARY COMPETITIVE ADAPTATIONS
1. **Hot ball player.** Players choosing a hot ball may serve and return a designated ball within their court and with their partner. This adaptation provides game-like stimulation for students with special needs who are not ready for fully inclusive play with a regulation ball.
2. **Crease player.** Players choosing to be assigned a crease area receive a zone, marked by cones, tape, or hoops, which represents their court space. This affords a student with special needs the opportunity to receive served balls in close proximity to their position. The crease limits the agility and speed required for competitive game play. The opponent may have a crease, or may have a regulation court space.
3. **Clock player.** Students choosing to be a clock player in tennis should be able to execute the serve in ten seconds or less. More than ten seconds delays the game and increases

player frustration. This option should be used when a player's skills require that he or she catch the ball before serving it over the net. This adaptation takes practice and patience by all players, and is best with the support of at least one engaged staff person.

PROGRESSIVE COMPETITIVE LEVELS SPORT SEQUENCE

Purpose: To provide structure to the positions and control to the pacing of the game.
 # Players: 2
Equipment: One tennis ball, regulation or improvised
Tennis net positioned regulation height or lower
Court boundaries highlighted with cones or flat discs
Clearly marked center line
Court numbers taped or chalked on court
At least one engaged staff member

Note: Students with special needs may participate using an inclusive activity at any progressive competitive level (PCL).

7-Level Tennis

Description: Students are paired with an ability-grouped partner, on either a standard or modified court. The equipment, including the net and ball, can be improvised or regulation, such that student success is maximized. The adaptations that follow involve modifications of the required skills (task), and both the court area and rules (environment). Students who are expected to participate in competitive tennis activities should begin by playing level 1 tennis. Once the majority of the students in the group have demonstrated mastery at level 1, they should be allowed to transition to level 2 play.

Students who have not mastered the skills for a particular level should be allowed to continue playing at their respective level while the remainder of the group moves to the next difficulty level. It is common to have students playing at different levels in the same class. For example, in any given class, Terrell is allowed to catch the ball before he serves it, while Maggie may be required to return the ball on one bounce.

Students may demonstrate mastery of level 1 or level 2 skills in a few minutes. The teacher should allow the students to progress when they demonstrate readiness, or the students will become frustrated and lose interest. Most intermediate classes progress through levels 1 and 2 in the introductory lesson. Most will progress through levels 3 and 4 during the second lesson. Ultimately, the majority of the students will reach their competitive limit at levels 4 or 5. By the conclusion of a tennis unit, a select few students play at levels 1, 2, or 3. The majority of the students play at levels 4 or 5, while some advanced players compete at levels 6 or 7. If the teacher develops the criteria for progressive levels appropriately, student performance should fit the standard bell curve parameters.

Level 1: Serve-Catch Tennis

1. One student serves underhand, much like badminton, such that the ball must travel over the net (net rule) and inside the court boundaries (line rule).
2. The server may position him or herself any distance from the net to get the ball over.
3. The receiver may not hit the ball, and must let the ball bounce to observe whether it is in or out of bounds. The receiver may catch the ball on the second bounce, or any thereafter.
4. If the ball travels over the net and bounces in bounds, the server does not "give" the receiver a point. If the server is unsuccessful, the receiver gets one point. Once the receiver catches the ball, he or she becomes a server.

5. The game continues until a player reaches a score of four points, or until the game proceeds for at least 10 serves, each without an error in serving.
6. Players who continue to serve without error are ready for level 2 tennis.

Level 2: Return Tennis

1. There is no serve in this game. Instead of serving, a player begins by underhand tossing a ball over the net such that it bounces inside the opponent's court boundaries.
2. The receiver must strike the ball with the racquet after it bounces such that the ball travels over the net and in bounds. Once the ball is hit, the original tosser must let the ball bounce to observe whether it lands in or out of bounds.
3. If the receiver makes a net or line error, he or she "gives" a point to the tosser.
4. The receiver then becomes the tosser, and the original tosser receives.
5. Game play continues until one player reaches four points, or until each player is able to return at least 10 balls without error.
6. Once each player is able to return 10 balls without error, he or she is ready for level 3 tennis.

Level 3: Rally Tennis

1. Level 3 tennis is a combination of levels 1 and 2 tennis.
2. The same player serves underhand the entire game. This must be explained and practiced, since levels 1 and 2 allowed alternating servers.
3. The one bounce rule applies, which states that the ball must bounce once before it is returned. It is an error to hit the ball in the air (volley), and to hit the ball if it bounces more than once.
4. The net rule and line rule apply as they did in levels 1 and 2.
5. The server must call the score verbally before each serve. An example is, "Two serving One." Reinforce this by awarding a point to the opponent if the score is not called.
6. The game ends when the first player reaches a score of four.
7. When students are able to play an entire game following the net, line, and bounce rules, as well as keep accurate score, they are ready for level 4 tennis.

Level 4: Official Scoring

1. All rules for level 3 apply except:
2. Regulation scoring terms are used. See diagram 9-1.
3. The first player to earn the fourth point wins. There is no deuce at this level.

Level 5: Deuce Tennis

1. Players should practice moving through the advantage-in/advantage-out floor model (diagram 9-2) to demonstrate understanding before game play.
2. All rules for level 4 apply except:
3. A four-to-four game is called deuce.
4. A player must win by two points.

Level 6: Tournament Tennis

1. All rules for level 5 apply except:
2. When a game ends, each player will play against a different partner.
3. While this level does not present cognitive or physical progression, it does provide a significant social progression. Many students have difficulty playing against a variety of partners. It is demanding socially and emotionally.

4. The replay rule is critical in terms of social and emotional development. If players disagree on a given point, the serve should be replayed and the score reset. A teacher should officiate if several points are replayed, as this rule is easily abused by manipulative students.

Diagram 9-3
Walker-Slider Tournament Rotation

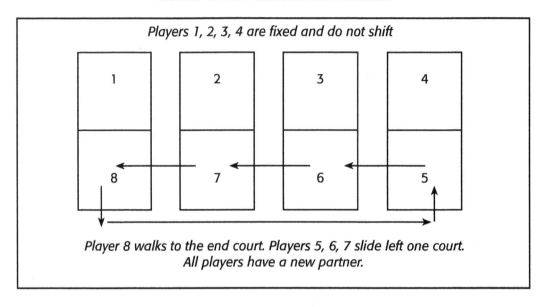

Diagram 9-4
Ladder Tournament Rotation

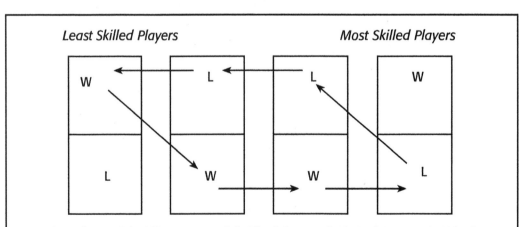

Level 7: Regulation Outdoor Tennis
1. Regulation game play.
2. Players are encouraged to serve overhand.
3. Strategy is emphasized.
4. Doubles partner-play may be included at this level.

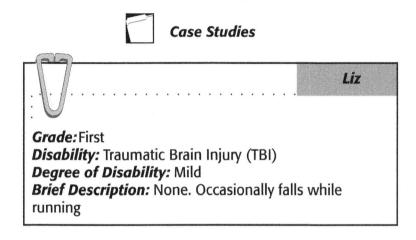

Case Studies

Liz

Grade: First
Disability: Traumatic Brain Injury (TBI)
Degree of Disability: Mild
Brief Description: None. Occasionally falls while running

Tennis Participation:

Liz enjoys net activities like tennis because she works well with partners. During the first lesson Liz works on underhand tossing and catching a partially deflated playground ball back and fourth under an arch with a friend. She also helps a classmate in a wheelchair practice the underhand serve skill using a beach ball. Her favorite individual activity includes hitting a foam tennis ball against the wall. She is able to rally the ball three times by the second lesson.

The teacher encourages Liz to work on underhand serving a Nerf ball, using her hand, with a partner. By the third lesson, Liz is able to use a paddle to hit foam tennis balls over a low net. She uses this skill to participate in a trashball game, and serve dozens of balls to the other team.

During preparatory activities, Liz excels at serving. She earns her racquetball racquet by the fifth lesson, and uses it to hit foam tennis balls back and fourth under the arch with a partner.

Liz is especially skilled serving tennis balls into the giant mat crater to bombard her classmates inside. By the end of the unit, Liz is able to rally a plastic pickleball back and forth over a net with a partner.

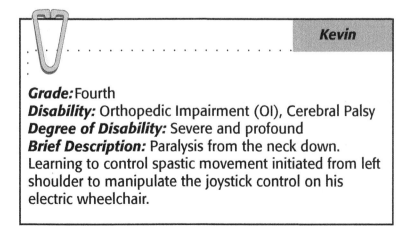

Kevin

Grade: Fourth
Disability: Orthopedic Impairment (OI), Cerebral Palsy
Degree of Disability: Severe and profound
Brief Description: Paralysis from the neck down. Learning to control spastic movement initiated from left shoulder to manipulate the joystick control on his electric wheelchair.

Tennis Participation:

Kevin is resistant to trying any of the tennis activities at first. That is, until he is introduced to the tennis video game. Kevin uses the game joystick just like his wheelchair controller to maneuver an electronic racquet to rally tennis balls. Not only is he successful—he is the envy of the class! This is one unit which everyone wanted to work with Kevin. This was especially beneficial for Kevin's self-esteem.

During future lessons, Kevin practices maneuvering the chute to roll tennis balls to a partner, and he masters pulling the tetherball over the net consistently.

One of Kevin's contributions in class is that he helps his classmates walk through the advantage-in/advantage-out floor model using verbal directions.

During tournament play, Kevin positions himself in a small crease marked by a giant hoola-hoop. Players rotating to Kevin's court play level 1 serving tennis. In this way, opponents need to serve accurately into Kevin's crease to earn a point. Kevin earns points when his opponent failed to serve into his crease. Kevin also returns the balls to his opponent using the chute. A peer-assistant helps Kevin pick up tennis balls and aim the chute.

Kevin starts the unit skeptically, but learns that through adaptation and improvisation, even tennis is not beyond his ability.

Maggie

Grade: Seventh
Disability: Orthopedic Impairment (OI), Cerebral Palsy
Degree of Disability: Moderate
Brief Description: Paraplegia affecting both legs, but not arms. Uses a wheelchair, walker, and/or quad canes, depending on the activity.

Tennis Participation:

Maggie chooses to skip the activities at the individual level and begin her work at the preparatory level. She excels at the warm-up games like wall-volleying. Maggie is able to hit the ball and wheel at the same time. Maggie tries all of the primary competitive adaptations during preparatory activities, and chooses to be a crease player for her first inclusive game. With each class Maggie is able to send the ball over the net with greater efficiency. By the end of the unit she is able to expand her crease to half the size of her classmates. This is significant in that she needs to move her wheelchair four feet in all directions to effectively return balls.

She spends a part of each class helping her more restricted peers who elect individual activities. She is particularly helpful teaching two students in wheelchairs the rules using a balloon for modified game-play.

During tournament play, Maggie chooses to challenge her opponents if they were willing to play in a wheelchair. She wins most of her tournament games, and finishes at the top of the "ladder rotation" (See Diagram 9-4).

Phil

Grade: Eleventh
Disability: Orthopedic Impairment (OI), Below Knee Amputee
Degree of Disability: Moderate
Brief Description: Phil is learning to use his newly fitted prosthesis, and chooses to use his wheelchair depending on the activity. He is athletic and competitive.

Tennis Participation:

Phil spends the first half of class participating with his prosthesis and the second half using his wheelchair. This gives his leg a much-needed chance to rest and recover from the workout. During warm-ups, Phil takes his time and walks through the activities. Phil chooses to play competitively, and does not like to use the primary competitive adaptations. His peers do not offer him any special privileges or favors, but he accommodates with good positioning and a slightly smaller court than his peers.

When Phil transitions to his chair, he officiates competitive games. Phil also spends a part of each class working at the preparatory level, practicing his serve and rally skills against the wall. Phil understands strategy needed for indoor tennis play, which compensates for his limited mobility. Phil participates at level 6 tennis—the highest level in the class. He looks forward to the challenge of playing on the outdoor court—level 7 tennis.

Chart 9-1:
Tennis Activities by Degree of Disability

	Mild	Moderate	Severe
Individual			
Catapult Tennis		X	X
Chute Tennis		X	X
Pulley Tennis		X	X
Air Hose Tennis		X	X
Pole Tennis		X	X
Crater Tennis		X	X
Preparatory			
Hot Ball Practice	X	X	X
Crease Practice	X	X	X
Clock Practice	X	X	
Inclusive			
Parachute Tennis	X	X	X
Scooter Tennis	X	X	X
Wheelchair Tennis	X	X	X
Keep It Up	X	X	X
Wall Ball Rally	X	X	X
Trashball Tennis	X	X	X
Mass Tennis	X	X	X
Crater Serving	X	X	X
PCL Levels 1-7	X	X	

CHAPTER 10

Baseball

Baseball is generally considered to be the "Great American Past-time," and many students are exposed to it in schools, recreational programs, and neighborhood parks. Unfortunately, as with so many other recreational activities, the more familiar the activity, the less likely providers are to make developmentally appropriate modifications when teaching. Students of all abilities deserve the chance to learn the game of baseball in a success-oriented environment. Many parents of children with special needs are interested in involving their children in recreational baseball leagues. If the adults running the program do not know how to adapt and improvise, read this chapter-and then show them how! For those professionals who find including students with special needs in baseball challenging, you are not alone. Baseball is so familiar, it is difficult to think of it in any other manner than the traditional way. As with all of our chapters, open your mind and climb out of your box-it is not so difficult once you adopt a few key modifications to the environment, the task, and the equipment.

ADAPTING THE ENVIRONMENT AND TASK

Cognitive Adaptations
1. **Base identification.** For small children, place identifiers at each base as follows:
   1st Base: A fuzzy stuffed animal-FUZZY FIRST.
   2nd Base: A rubber snake-SLIMY SECOND.
   3rd Base: A water bottle-THIRSTY THIRD.
   Home Plate: Staff or student-HIGH-FIVES AT HOME.
   For older students, label the bases with a marker, and position a cone at each base with the number it represents.
2. **Boundary highlights.** Use cones to mark the fair-foul lines. Chalk outdoor fields to highlight the boundary.
3. **Bench dug-out.** Students need a safe place to sit while waiting to bat. Students with attention deficits will need specific directions and clear limits during this "wait time."
4. **Bat-a-round inning.** Explain that an inning ends when each player has batted once. The exception is if the batting team receives three outs. This is obviously a strategy to facilitate equity and fairness with respect to the time constraints of many programs who do not have two or more hours for regulation gameplay.
5. **Force-out rule.** Students need to know when they may be "forced out." During the learning phase, each runner should be reminded in between pitches whether they are a "force-out" player or a "tag out" player. Fielders use the reminder as well.

6. *Tag-out rule.* Students need to know when they are a "tag out" player. Fielders use the reminder as well.

7. *Special circumstances/teachable moments.* Beginning players should not be bombarded with the intricacies of the game. Just as the "back-court" rule in basketball can wait until a certain level of gameplay proficiency is reached, so too, may baseball rules such as: the infield fly rule, tagging up, leading off, bunting, pitcher balks, picking off runners, sliding...etc.

Affective Adaptations

1. *No strike outs.* Students may not strike out in our lower level games. After two strikes are earned, students are afforded the choice of tossing the ball to him or herself, or using the batting tee from which to hit. If two strikes are earned by tossing, then the player hits from the tee. The player swings until the ball is hit. More advanced players who may handle the emotional stress of striking out may elect to be a three-strike player.

2. *Teach the tag out.* Players need to see what a tag out looks like and feels like. Explain that the ball may tag a player out, or the glove if the ball is in the glove. Be sure to explain that a ball may not be thrown at a player to tag them out, as in the game of kick ball.

3. *Ability-group teams.* Avoid traditional "team-captain" selection of teams. Inevitably the same students will consistently be picked last. Instead, adopt the routine of "ability grouping." This technique involves allowing students to pair themselves with a player of comparable ability. The partners then select opposite color jerseys and move to their respective areas. Teams will then be automatically "even" in terms of ability. In the case of an uneven number of students, the single player should partner with staff. This means that the staff person will need to be actively engaged in game play. If there is only one teacher, the single student may consider rotating into game play with a group of three.

4. *Staff pitcher.* Students need a consistent, responsible person to pitch balls. Once students trust the pitcher, they may elect to receive underhand or overhand pitches. Adult staff control the entire game from the pitcher's mound. Staff should use this position to provide: verbal directions, reminders, instruction, praise and reinforcement, as well as fielding plays. If a peer opponent pitches, empower the batter to request a staff pitcher if safety, maturity, or control become issues.

5. *Inner and outer baseline.* A faster player will likely become frustrated by a slower moving runner. Create a parallel baseline around the diamond for slower moving runners, and students using assistive devices. This allows faster runners to pass slower players. All rules apply for runners on the inner and outer loop respectively. This requires two first bases, two second bases, two third bases, and two home plates.

6. *Limited catcher-rule.* Players should not catch behind home plate, unless they have all the appropriate safety equipment which is in good repair and fits properly-many programs fall short in this area. If this is the case, allow a player to act as a catcher only to provide fielding and plays at the plate. Batters should retrieve their own missed pitches.

Sensorimotor Adaptations

1. *Beeper balls.* Beeper balls are usually made of foam and have an electronic beeping mechanism inserted into a cylinder shaped cavity. When the beeper is activated, it sounds a repetitive tone that visually impaired students use to track and locate balls. Beeper balls work well as hot balls during inclusive game play.

2. *Nerf balls.* Students who are visually impaired are vulnerable to being struck by equipment during class. Teacher judgment is critical to minimize the risk of baseballs striking visually impaired students. Soft balls should be used during inclusive activities to minimize the risk of injury.

3. **Raised bases.** Raised bases may be placed on the floor or field to create a type of "Braille" play surface.
4. **Running buddy.** Visually impaired students may run around the bases with a sighted partner.
5. **Safety buddy.** A buddy may be assigned to protect visually impaired students from being struck by airborne balls.
6. **Scoring.** Score should be shown visually and called verbally to assist students with hearing and vision impairments.

IMPROVISING EQUIPMENT

As discussed in Part I, psychomotor modifications occur through the process of improvising the equipment and facility. The following modifications are introduced relative to three categories of equipment-traditional, alternative, and fabricated.

Traditional Equipment
1. **Inner and outer loop bases.** A faster player will likely become frustrated by a slower moving runner. Create a parallel baseline around the diamond for slower moving runners, and students using assistive devices. This allows faster runners to pass slower players. All rules apply for runners on the inner and outer loop respectively. This requires two first bases, two second bases, two third bases, and two home plates.
2. **Bats.** Include a variety of weights and lengths of plastic, wood, and aluminum bats.
3. **Baseballs.** The key here is LIMITED FLIGHT BALLS. There are several available commercially such as "the only ball," and the "incrediball." Limited flight balls provide realistic action off the bat, however they fly only half as far as traditional hard baseballs. Fielders may catch these balls with gloves or bare-handed, as they are lighter and less dense than traditional balls. If space is limited, these balls are the answer to providing realistic game-play in restricted areas.
4. **Gloves.** Clearly label gloves for left handed players and right handed players. Remember, beginners will be confused by wearing a glove on their non-dominant hand. Explain that their strong hand should be free with which to throw.

Alternative Equipment
1. **Pitcher's crate.** Beginners need a concrete signal indicating when to stop running around the bases. Explain that when fielders place the ball inside the crate all runners must stop.
2. **Wheelchairs.** Able-bodied students may elect to participate in an inclusive game of wheelchair baseball. As with scooters, the experience will facilitate an awareness of the challenges associated with a disabling condition.
3. **Beach balls.** Beach balls are lightweight, colorful, and have a special feature which few teachers utilize-the inflation stem. When pulled outward, the stem provides a handy appendage from which students can pick up, carry, and release. This is particularly helpful for students who are limited in their ability to reach from their wheelchair, cane, or walker. The stem is also helpful for underhand serving. Students hold the ball by the stem with one hand, and strike with the other.
4. **Tennis racquets.** Students with difficulty hitting pitched balls may be successful with the wide head of a tennis racquet. Be sure to pitch light weight balls, such as tennis balls, beach balls, or foam balls, as hard baseballs will damage the racquet.

Fabricated Equipment
1. **PVC chute.** See Part I for description. The chute provides a student-controlled path along which balls may reach a designated goal. The chute may be used to send balls into the field

in place of batting. Students who bat with a chute move to first base automatically, without risk of being out. They may be put out once the next batter hits.

2. **Catapult.** See Part I for description. The Catapult allows students to mechanically launch balls with minimal physical effort. This adaptation works well indoors with a homerun derby set-up in which the distance the ball travels determines bases and runs.

3. **The pole.** The teacher holds the pole, much like a fishing pole, with a lightweight ball attached to the pole by a length of cord. The teacher uses the pole to "hover" the ball in front of the student, making it easier to hit. A ball held by a clothes pin will break away and act as a batted ball. This works well when a wiffle ball is batted by a tennis racquet.

IPI INCLUSION MODEL

Individual Activities

Baseball may be thought of as a thematic game involving hitting a ball and traveling around bases to score points. Keeping this loose framework in mind, we develop activities that allow students to participate in activities that they can master individually, at their developmental levels. Students who master these activities may choose to participate in more advanced and "game-like" preparatory activities. Get out of your box and keep an open mind! Students love these activities.

1. **Catapult baseball.** Position the catapult such that a student can drop a bat or glove onto the raised arm of the lever. Position the fulcrum so the catapulted object (tennis balls work well) is launched into the field. This adaptation works well indoors with a homerun derby set-up in which the distance the ball travels determines bases and runs.

2. **Chute baseball.** (Resembles a bowling lane gutter) The chute may be used by batters to send balls into the field. The chute may be used by fielders to send the ball to the pitcher to stop runners from advancing.

Preparatory Activities

By definition, the nature of these activities prepares students for participation in the inclusive activity. Therefore, any activity that prepares a student for participation with the main body of the class may be considered preparatory. Students typically need practice selecting which primary competitive adaptation is best for them. They also need practice with small groups of peers at this level of participation.

1. **Hot ball practice.** The student gains familiarity with his or her selected ball by catching, tossing, and striking it individually.

2. **Crease practice.** The crease in baseball related activities is the inner loop baseline. This inner-loop allows students who move slower to move at their own pace. It also distinguishes students who elect modified batting options. See primary competitive adaptations section.

3. **Clock practice.** The clock assists batters by providing the student a period of time in which fielders may not move or touch the ball. This may range from 3-10 seconds of "free" transition time from home plate to first base.

4. **The fielding crate.** Students with special needs may have a crate near their position. Fielders may choose to throw, roll, or hand the ball to the student with special needs, who may then drop the ball into the crate-which causes all runners to stop at the last base touched.

Inclusive Activities
Recreational and Leadup Activities

1. **Kickball.** A baseball like game in which students kick instead of bat, and fielders may hit runners for a put-out.

2. *Ghostbusters.* Each student places a bowling pin (ghost) on the floor, and uses his or her feet to protect the pin from being knocked down by soccer balls. Nerf-type soccer balls are positioned all over the gym floor. Students choose the best time to leave their pins unprotected so they may kick a ball toward another player's pin. If a player's pin is knocked down (busted) then the player needs to execute a designated number of exercises to "re-energize" their "ghost," (reset their pin). The game ends after a set duration of time.

3. *Homerun derby.* A batting game in which a batter earns bases by the distance a batted ball flies. The field is marked to designate singles, doubles, triples, homeruns, and grand slams.

4. *Run down.* A small group game in which runners are positioned at one of two bases. One fielder is positioned at each base. Runners attempt to move from one base to the other without being tagged out. Tagged players become "enders" at the base where he or she was tagged.

5. *Three flys.* A fielding game in which a group of students are positioned in the outfield. A batter hits from a self-toss. Any fly ball entering a fielder's "zone" may be caught in the air. Once three flys are caught, the fielder becomes the batter.

6. *Never out.* An aerobic game in which a batter hits the ball and runs the bases. The fielders must perform a cooperative task to make the runner stop. A sample task might require all players to touch the ball to make the runner stop. Each time the runner touches home plate a run is scored for his or her team. When the second batter, hits, he or she runs with the first batter in a cumulative fashion. If there are ten players, there will be ten players running the bases following the tenth player's at-bat. A scorekeeper is required to tally the runs which accumulate quickly! The fittest students should bat first, as they will run the longest. A signal should be sounded to ensure the runners stop in a timely manner.

PRIMARY COMPETITIVE ADAPTATIONS

1. *Hot ball player.* Players choosing a hot ball or hot bat may bat a ball or field a ball other than the game ball used by the main body of the class. This adaptation provides game-like stimulation for students with special needs who are not ready for fully inclusive play.

2. *Crease player.* Players choosing to run on the inner-loop baseline have an area in which they can move around the bases at their own pace. Fielders who elect a crease area are assigned a fielding crate. If a crease player receives a ball from a teammate, it may be placed in the crate to stop runners from advancing.

3. *Clock player.* The clock assists batters by providing the student a period of time in which fielders may not move or touch the ball. This may range from 3-10 seconds of "free" transition time from home plate to first base.

Batting Options

Option A: Choose a Pinch Hitter. A peer will hit for the student, however the student must travel the inner loop bases, and may be out at first base.

Option B: Choose a Pinch Runner. A peer will run the bases after the student with special needs hits the ball. If the pinch runner makes it safely to a base, the student with special needs starts at that point on the inner loop before the next batter hits. The pinch runner returns to the dug-out once the student transitions to the correct base.

Option C: Automatic First. The student with special needs wants to hit and run, however past performance has shown it is very likely that he or she will be out at first base. The student may bat, or use the chute, and then transition to first base automatically. He or she may be put out at any other base starting with the next batter.

PROGRESSIVE COMPETITIVE LEVELS SPORT SEQUENCE

Purpose: To provide structure to the positions and control to the pacing of the game.
 # Players: 8-12 players per team, two teams
Equipment: One regulation or adapted baseball
Two baselines: inner and outer loop
Baselines marked with cones, tape, or chalk
Clearly designated dug-out area
Bases labeled and highlighted with cones
Colored jerseys for each team
At least one engaged staff member
Batting tee and fielding crate

3-Level Baseball

Description: Students are arranged in baseball formation, on either a standard or modified court or field. The equipment, including the bat and balls, can be improvised or regulation, such that student success is maximized. The adaptations that follow involve modifications of the required skills (task), and both the field area and rules (environment). Students who are expected to participate in competitive baseball activities should begin by playing level 1 baseball. Once the majority of the students in the group have demonstrated mastery at level 1, they should be allowed to transition to level 2 play.

Students who have not mastered the skills for a particular level should be allowed to continue playing at their respective level while the remainder of the group moves to the next difficulty level. It is common to have groups of students playing at different levels in the same class. For example, in any given game Terrell chooses to have a pinch hitter, while Maggie hits and fields according to regulation rules.

Students may demonstrate mastery of level 1 or level 2 skills in the first class. The teacher should allow the students to progress when they demonstrate readiness, or the students will become frustrated and lose interest. Most intermediate classes progress through level 1 in the introductory lesson. Most will progress to level 2 during the remaining lessons. By the conclusion of a baseball unit, a select few students play at level 1. The majority of the students play at level 2, while some advanced players compete at level 3. If the teacher develops the criteria for progressive levels appropriately, student performance should fit the standard bell curve parameters.

Level 1: Baseball (Limited Skills and Limited Game-Time)

1. Staff pitches underhand only.
2. Students may not strike out. The toss or tee rule applies.
3. The inning ends after each player has a turn at-bat, regardless of outs.
4. Fielders may stop runners by placing the ball in a fielder's crate.
5. Staff govern the game pace and climate with active participation.
6. Fun and participation is emphasized.

Level 2: Baseball (Intermediate Skills)

1. Staff or students may pitch. Batter may elect a staff pitcher. Batter may elect underhand or overhand pitching, as well as speed (slow, medium, fast).
2. Batters may elect to be a three-strike player, in which they may strike out at bat.
3. The inning ends after each player bats or three outs-whichever comes first.
4. Fielders may stop runners by throwing the ball to the pitcher.
5. Game rules are presented during teachable moments-i.e. infield fly rule.
6. Staff foster sportsmanship and facilitate student leadership by modeling positive examples.
7. Learning and the play process is emphasized.

Level 3: Baseball (Advanced Skills)

1. Peers pitch underhand or overhand.
2. Batters are out after three strikes.
3. The inning ends after three outs.
4. Fielders may only stop runners by tag out or force out.
5. Rules are expected to be known.
6. Students take an active role generating a positive climate, with positive cheering and sportsmanship.
7. Strategy and technique is emphasized.

Case Studies

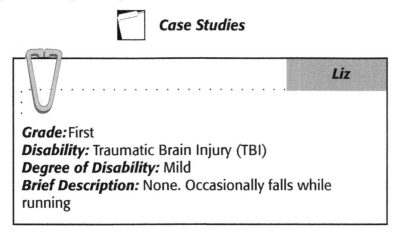

Liz

Grade: First
Disability: Traumatic Brain Injury (TBI)
Degree of Disability: Mild
Brief Description: None. Occasionally falls while running

Baseball Participation:

Liz enjoys being outside, and base activities mean spring has arrived! She spends the first few lessons working with her peers who use wheelchairs. She helps the students with the individual activities like chute baseball and catapult baseball. The teacher encourages Liz to work on batting pitched balls with a partner. She is most successful hitting balls suspended from the tether pole.

During preparatory activities, Liz excels at kicking a stationary ball and running around the bases. Her favorite lead-up game is never out, and she really gets a workout moving around the bases continuously. By the end of the unit, Liz is able to play in a wiffleball game that included fielding using several fielder's crates.

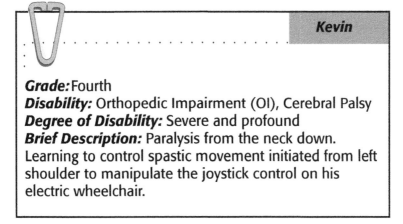

Kevin

Grade: Fourth
Disability: Orthopedic Impairment (OI), Cerebral Palsy
Degree of Disability: Severe and profound
Brief Description: Paralysis from the neck down. Learning to control spastic movement initiated from left shoulder to manipulate the joystick control on his electric wheelchair.

Baseball Participation:

Kevin begins his first lesson practicing both his catapult and chute options for batting. Neither seems to motivate Kevin, as he wants to participate in a more game-like way. By the second class, one group of students are already playing level one baseball, and Kevin joins in. He elects the pinch hitter batting option, and travels around the inner loop of the bases. In the field, Kevin plays using a crate on the ground by his chair. Teammates who field balls place them on Kevin's armrest such that he can knock the into his crate and stop the runners from advancing.

During the unit, his classmates progressed to level 2 baseball. Kevin continues to participate using his adaptations.

Maggie

Grade: Seventh
Disability: Orthopedic Impairment (OI), Cerebral Palsy
Degree of Disability: Moderate
Brief Description: Paraplegia affecting both legs, but not arms. Uses a wheelchair, walker, and/or quad canes, depending on the activity.

Baseball Participation:

Maggie chooses to skip the activities at the individual level and begin her work at the preparatory level. She excels at the lead-up games like home-run derby and run-down. Maggie works during the first few lessons choosing a bat and ball combination that gives her the best chance of getting on base. She ultimately chooses a tennis racquet, and a tennis ball pitched underhand.

Maggie tries all of the primary competitive adaptations during preparatory activities, and chooses to be a crease player, using the inner loop base-line for her first inclusive game. By the end of the unit she is able to hit the tennis ball with such force, she has time to use her walker to transition to first base independently!

Although she enjoys baseball on the grass, she reports she would rather use her wheelchair playing on the hard court surface, because it is less tiring.

Phil

Grade: Eleventh
Disability: Orthopedic Impairment (OI), Below Knee Amputee
Degree of Disability: Moderate
Brief Description: Phil is learning to use his newly fitted prosthesis, and chooses to use his wheelchair depending on the activity. He is athletic and competitive.

Baseball Participation:

Phil spends the first half of class participating with his prosthesis, and the second half using his wheelchair. This gives his leg a much-needed chance to rest and recover from the workout. During warm-ups, Phil takes his time and walks through the activities. Phil chooses to play competitively, and does not like to use the primary competitive adaptations. His peers do not offer him any special privileges or favors, but he accommodates with good batting and fielding skills. When Phil transitions to his chair, he umpires competitive games. Phil also spends a part of each class working at the preparatory level, practicing his batting and fielding with a partner. Phil has the skill to play baseball on a recreation league, once he develops more tolerance for his prosthesis.

Chart 10-1:
Baseball Activities by Degree of Disability

	Mild	Moderate	Severe
Individual			
Catapult Baseball		X	X
Chute Baseball		X	X
Preparatory			
Hot Ball Practice	X	X	X
Crease Practice	X	X	X
Clock Practice	X	X	X
Fielding Crate Practice	X	X	
Inclusive			
Kickball	X	X	X
Ghostbusters	X	X	X
Homerun Derby	X	X	X
Run-Down	X	X	X
3-Flys	X	X	X
Never-Out	X	X	X
PCL Levels 1-3	X	X	

References

American Psychiatric Association. (1994). *Diagnostic and statistical manual of mental disorders: DSM IV* 4th ed. Washington, D.C.: American Psychiatric Association.

Block, M.E. (1992). What is appropriate physical education for students with profound disabilities? *Adapted Physical Activity Quarterly, 9,* 197-213.

Connolly, P., & Peterson, C. (1978). *Characteristics of special populations.* Hawkins & Associates, 804 "D" St. N.E., Washington, D.C.

Dattilo, J. (1994). *Inclusive leisure services: Responding to the rights of people with disabilities.* State College, PA: Venture Publishing.

DeLoach, C., & Greer, G. (1981). *Adjustment to severe physical disability.* New York: McGraw-Hill Book Company.

Gallahue, D.L. (1987). *Developmental physical education for today's elementary school children.* New York: Macmillan.

Gallahue, & Ozmun. (1998). *Understanding motor development: Infants, children, adolescents, adults.* Boston: WCB/McGraw Hill.

Geddes D. (1974). *Physical activities for individuals with handicapping conditions.* St. Louis: Mosby.

Hardman, M. et. al. (1990). *Human exceptionality* (3rd ed.) Boston: Allyn & Bacon.

Haring, N., & McCormack, L. (Eds.). (1990). *Exceptional children and youth.* Columbus, OH: Merrill Publishing Company.

Heward, W., & Orlansky, M. (1988). *Exceptional children.* Columbus, OH: Merrill Publishing Company.

Hutchison, P., & McGill, J. (1992). *Leisure, integration, and community.* Concord, Ontario: Leisurability Publications, Inc.

Kennedy, D., Smith, R., & Austin, D. (1991). *Special recreation: Opportunities for persons with disabilities.* Dubuque, IA: William C. Brown, Publishers.

Kirk, S., & Gallagher, J. (1989). *Educating exceptional children.* Boston: Houghton Mifflin Company.

Neulinger, J. (1981). *The psychology of leisure.* (2nd ed.). Springfield, IL: Charles C. Thomas, Publisher.

Reid, G. (1993). Motor behavior and individuals with disabilities: Linking research and practice. *Adapted Physical Activity Quarterly, 10,* 359-370.

Schleien, S.J., Olson, K.D., Rodgers, N.C., & McLafferty, M.E. (1985). Integrating children with severe handicaps into recreation and physical education programs. *Journal of Park and Recreation Administration, 3(1),* 50-66.

Wehman, P., & Schleien, S. (1981). *Leisure programs for handicapped persons: Adaptations, techniques, and curriculum.* Baltimore: University Park Press.

Internet Sites

1. flaghouse.com (Adapted Physical Education Equipment Catalog)
2. sportime.com (Adapted Physical Education Equipment Catalog)
3. twu.edu./apens/ (Adapted Physical Education National Standards)
4. palaestra.com (Adapted Sports Magazine)
5. uscpaa.org (U.S. Cerebral Palsy Athletic Association)
6. wheelchairsportsinc.com (Wheelchair Sports & Recreation Association)
7. nsnsports.org (National Sports Network)
8. gotocrystal.net/leep/ (Leisure Education for Exceptional People)
9. challengedathletes.org (Challenged Athletes Foundation)
10. geocel.com (Assistive Devices Company)
11. assis-tech.com (Assistive Devices Company)
12. wings.buffalo.edu (Center for Assistive Technology)
13. blackberrytech.com (Assistive Technology Company)
14. wheelchairparts.com (Wheelchair parts & accessories)

Special Equipment

The Any-Pole Basketball Goal. Mast Corporation. 4105 Underwood Rd. Baltimore, MD. 21218. 1.800.642.4522.

Index

A

adapting the environment and task
    in baseball, 87–89
    in basketball, 37–38
    creating developmentally appropriate
        activities by, 24
    dynamic vs. static play environments,
        23
    open-skill vs. closed-skill tasks, 23–24
    in soccer, 61–62
    in tennis, 73–75
    in volleyball, 49–50
    see also Primary Competitive
        Adaptations (PCA)
affective domain, 12
age, and sports skills, 18
arches, 31
autism/pervasive developmental disability
    (PDD), 8

B

baseball
    activities by degree of disability, 95
    adapting the environment and task, 87–
        89
    affective adaptations, 88
    applying the IPI inclusion model, 90–91
    applying the progressive-competitive-
        levels (PCL) strategy, 92–93
    cognitive adaptations, 87–88
    importance of developmentally
        appropriate modifications, 87
    improvising with alternative equipment,
        89
    improvising with fabricated equipment,
        89–90
    improvising with traditional equipment,
        89
    inclusive recreational and lead-up
        activities, 90–91
    individual activities, 90
    participation case studies, 93–94
    preparatory activities, 90
    primary competitive adaptations (PCA),
        91
    sensorimotor adaptations, 88–89
    3-Level, 92–93
basketball
    activities by degree of disability, 48
    adaptability of, 37
    adapting the environment and task, 37–
        38
    affective adaptations, 38
    applying the IPI inclusion model, 41–43
    applying the progressive-competitive-
        levels (PCL) strategy, 43–45
    cognitive adaptations, 37–38
    improvising with alternative equipment,
        39–40
    improvising with fabricated equipment,
        40
    improvising with traditional equipment,
        39
    inclusive lead-up activities, 42–43
    inclusive recreational activities, 42
    individual activities, 41
    participation case studies, 45–47
    preparatory activities, 41–42
    primary competitive adaptations (PCA),
        43
    sensorimotor adaptations, 38
    6-Level, 43–45

C

catapults, 32
change, cycle of. see cycle of change
chutes, 30
claws, 32–33
clock concept, 26–27
closed-skill tasks, 23–24
cognitive domain
    example of cognitive adaptation, 11–12
    teaching students vs. lessons, 11
    using the VAKT approach, 11
content expertise, 15

crease concept, 25–26
cycle of change
  responsibility of staff to "sell"
    alternative rules, 21
  stages in, 20
  working through student resistance, 20–
    21

D
disability, degrees of
  mild, 8–9
  moderate, 9–10
  severe, 10
domains, educational. *see* educational
  domains
dynamic play environments, 23

E
educational domains
  affective, 12
  cognitive, 11–12
  psychomotor, 12–13
  sensorimotor, 13
emotionally disturbed (ED), 8
environment, adapting the. *see* adapting the
  environment and task
equipment, improvising
  alternative equipment, 29
  in baseball, 89–90
  in basketball, 39–40
  fabricated equipment, 29–34
  in soccer, 63–64
  in tennis, 75–77
  traditional equipment, 29
  in volleyball, 51–52

F
fabricated equipment, universal
  application in specific sports, 34
  arch, 31
  catapult, 32
  chute, 30
  claw, 32–33
  pole, 30–31
  pulley, 31–32
  reasons for making, 29–30
  using PVC pipe, 33
Federal Handicapping Conditions
  autism/pervasive developmental
    disability (PDD), 8
  emotionally disturbed (ED), 8
  hearing impaired (HI), 8, 9, 10
  learning disabled (LD), 7–8
  multi-disabled (MD), 7, 9, 10
  orthopedically impaired (OI), 7, 9, 10

other health impaired (OHI), 8, 9, 10
traumatically brain injured (TBI), 7, 9,
  10
visually impaired (VI), 8, 9, 10

G
grouping students, 5

H
handicapping conditions. *see* Federal
  Handicapping Conditions
hearing impaired (HI)
  definition of, 8
  mild disability, 9
  moderate disability, 10
hot concept, 25

I
inclusive level, IPI inclusion model, 17–18
Individual, Preparatory, Inclusive (IPI)
  inclusion model
    in baseball, 90–91
    in basketball, 41–43
    diagram of, 15
    inclusive level, 17–18
    individual level, 16
    preparatory level, 16–17
    in soccer, 64–66
    in tennis, 77–79
    in volleyball, 52–55
individual level, IPI inclusion model, 16
input-output principle, 32

L
learning disabled (LD), 7–8

M
mild disabilities
  case study examples, 9
  definition of, 8
moderate disabilities
  case study examples, 9–10
  definition of, 9
multi-disabled (MD)
  definition of, 7
  mild disability, 9
  moderate disability, 10

O
open-skill tasks, 23
orthopedically impaired (OI)
  definition of, 7
  mild disability, 9
  moderate disability, 9
  severe disability, 10

other health impaired (OHI)
    definition of, 8
    mild disability, 9
    moderate disability, 10

P
pervasive developmental disability (PDD)/
    autism, 8
physical education
    as a collaborative effort between special
        and regular educators, 5–6
    content *vs.* process expertise, 15
poles, 30–31
preparatory level, IPI inclusion model, 16–17
Primary Competitive Adaptations (PCA)
    in baseball, 91
    in basketball, 43
    clock concept, 26–27
    crease concept, 25–26
    definition and purpose of, 24
    hot concept, 25
    making adaptations available to all
        students, 24
    presenting adaptations positively, 26
    in soccer, 67
    in tennis, 79–80
    in volleyball, 55
process expertise, 15
Progressive-Competitive-Levels (PCL)
    strategy
        in baseball, 92–93
        in basketball, 43–45
        definition of, 18
        example of, 18–20
        in soccer, 67–69
        sports-skills competencies as age related
            vs. age dependent, 18
        in tennis, 80–83
        in volleyball, 55–57
psychomotor domain
    examples of psychomotor adaptation,
        12–13
    scope of, 12
pulleys, 31–32
PVC pipe, 33

R
resistance to change, working through, 20–
    21

S
segregation, physical disability, 4–5
sensorimotor domain, 13
7-Level Soccer, 67–69
7-Level Tennis, 80–83
7-Level Volleyball, 18–20, 55–57

severe disabilities, 10
6-Level Basketball, 43–45
soccer
    activities by degree of disability, 72
    adapting the environment and task, 61–
        62
    affective adaptations, 62
    as an invasive sport, 61
    applying the IPI inclusion model, 64–66
    applying the progressive-competitive-
        levels (PCL) strategy, 67–69
    cognitive adaptations, 61–62
    extra challenges of, 61
    improvising with alternative equipment,
        63–64
    improvising with fabricated equipment,
        64
    improvising with traditional equipment,
        63
    inclusive lead-up activities, 66
    inclusive recreational activities, 65–66
    individual activities, 64–65
    participation case studies, 69–72
    preparatory activities, 65
    primary competitive adaptations (PCA),
        67
    sensorimotor adaptations, 62
    7-Level, 67–69
static play environments, 23
students with disabilities, attitudes toward,
    3–5

T
task, adapting the. *see* adapting the
    environment and task
tennis
    activities by degree of disability, 86
    adapting the environment and task, 73–
        75
    affective adaptations, 75
    applying the IPI inclusion model, 77–79
    applying the progressive-competitive-
        levels (PCL) strategy, 80–83
    challenges of teaching, 73
    cognitive adaptations, 73–75
    importance of proper instructions and
        practice, 73
    improvising with alternative equipment,
        76–77
    improvising with fabricated equipment,
        77
    improvising with traditional equipment,
        75–76
    inclusive recreational and lead-up
        activities, 79
    individual activities, 77–78

participation case studies, 83–85
preparatory activities, 78
primary competitive adaptations (PCA), 79–80
sensorimotor adaptations, 75
7-Level, 80–83
3-Level Baseball, 92–93
traumatically brain injured (TBI)
    definition of, 7
    mild disability, 9
    moderate disability, 10

V
VAKT approach to teaching, 11
visually impaired (VI)
    definition of, 8
    mild disability, 9
    moderate disability, 10
volleyball
    activities by degree of disability, 60
    adapting the environment and task, 49–50
    affective adaptations, 50
    applying the IPI inclusion model, 52–55
    applying the progressive-competitive-
        levels (PCL) strategy, 55–57
    cognitive adaptations, 49–50
    importance of presenting in developmentally appropriate stages, 49
    improvising with alternative equipment, 51–52
    improvising with fabricated equipment, 52
    improvising with traditional equipment, 51
    inclusive lead-up activities, 54–55
    inclusive recreational activities, 54
    individual activities, 52–53
    participation case studies, 57–59
    preparatory activities, 53
    primary competitive adaptations (PCA), 55
    sensorimotor adaptations, 50
    7-Level, 55–57
    versatility of, 49

W
whole child philosophy, 11–13